Anonymous

Sheep and Pigs, and Other Live Stock

a complete guide to the breeding and rearing of sheep, pigs, goats, asses

and mules : with illustrations

Anonymous

Sheep and Pigs, and Other Live Stock
*a complete guide to the breeding and rearing of sheep, pigs, goats, asses and mules
: with illustrations*

ISBN/EAN: 9783337741952

Printed in Europe, USA, Canada, Australia, Japan

Cover: Foto ©Andreas Hilbeck / pixelio.de

More available books at **www.hansebooks.com**

SHEEP AND PIGS,

AND

OTHER LIVE STOCK.

A

COMPLETE GUIDE TO THE BREEDING AND REARING

OF

SHEEP, PIGS, GOATS, ASSES, AND MULES.

With Illustrations.

London:

WARD, LOCK AND CO.,

WARWICK HOUSE, SALISBURY SQUARE, E.C.

PUBLISHERS' PREFACE.

THE following work, forming one of our series of handbooks in which all matters relating to rural life are carefully and popularly treated, deals with a considerable portion of the live stock of the farm.

Sheep, Pigs, Goats, Asses, and Mules, are here spoken of in turn, and such particulars are given regarding the management of these animals, as, if attended to, will certainly secure success to all who take the rearing of them in hand.

Sheep and Pigs, on account of their importance, have naturally had the greater portion of our space allotted to them; but the smaller share of attention devoted to the other animals will, we believe, be found sufficient for all practical purposes.

The author, who is a farmer of experience, has had in view not only those who carry on farming operations on an extensive scale, but others in a small way of business, and he hopes that his work will not come amiss even to the cottager who possesses but a single pig, or who strives, by the keeping of a few sheep, to make a sensible addition to his earnings.

For one or two of our illustrations we are indebted to Messrs. Bayliss, Jones and Bayliss, Wolverhampton; the St. Pancras Iron Work Company, London, N.W.; and Messrs. Ransomes, Sims and Head, Ipswich.

LIST OF ILLUSTRATIONS.

CONTENTS.

SHEEP, PIGS, GOATS, ASSES, AND MULES.

CHAPTER I.

BREEDS AND VARIETIES OF SHEEP.

Natural History—Colonial Wool—Breeds and Varieties—The Merino Sheep—English Sheep — Long-wool — Short-wool—Leicester Sheep — Five-year-old Mutton—Lincoln Sheep—Southdown Sheep—Weights per Quarter of Different Sheep.

1. **NATURAL HISTORY.**—Sheep have played a very important part in the annals of modern British husbandry, as well as in commerce, and the consumption of wool is now enormous. London of late years has also become a depôt for colonial wools, the annual series of sales· which are held at the Wool Exchange, in Coleman Street, attracting thither not only native consumers, but a large number of buyers from the Continent, who compete in the most spirited manner for the best lots with home purchasers especially the representatives of French and German houses. In the case of the latter, much of the wool is returned to us again in

B

the shape of yarns, some particular kinds of which—as that known as *vigonia*, for instance—they excel the British manufacturer in producing; while in the case of France, a large quantity of the wool so re-exported from England, that first came from the Australian and other colonies, is returned to England in the shape of all wool dress-goods that are turned out at Roubaix, which may be considered the Manchester of France.

In one month, that of September, 1879, the re-exports of wool were 36,000,000 lbs.; the money value of the same amounting to £2,101,000; which will give some idea of the magnitude of the trade.

The comparatively modern method of farming upon the principle known as the "turnip system of husbandry," by which large numbers of sheep are maintained on the land that is planted with turnips and other green crops for their support, has effected quite a revolution in the old plan upon which English agriculture used to be conducted. Formerly, after grain crops had been taken off the land, it was allowed to lie a bare fallow until it had recovered itself from the amount of exhaustion it had undergone, or until it came again into "heart," as it was termed; but by means of the proper rotation of crops—that is understood better than formerly, and which enables a large quantity of stock to be kept upon the land, whose manure enriches it—under the hands of a clever agriculturist, very little time is now lost in bare fallows; and the land gives forth its increase in a much more unstinted manner than under the old system of farming.

2. COLONIAL WOOL.—The growth of the Australian wool trade affords one of the most illustrative examples possible of the results that are to be derived from suitable pasturage adapted to the race of sheep that are placed thereon, or which are indigenous to it; and the history of the growth of the Australian wool trade is both interesting and remarkable.

Botany Bay was formed into a penal settlement, and our convicts were first sent there in 1788, in accordance with the legislative views then entertained as to the best disposal of them; and to supply the young colony with mutton and wool, some small hairy sheep were imported from Bengal; and these, although not by any means a thrifty race, improved to such a marked degree that it was soon seen that the soil and climate of the country was peculiarly well fitted for sheep-farming, and small numbers of some of the best breeds of sheep were procured from England; amongst others, Leicesters and Southdowns.

At first the business was managed by persons who did not follow it out with all the care and attention to details which breeders are in the habit of giving to what they undertake, and a good deal of it was necessarily performed in a slovenly, and eareless manner; yet, notwithstanding, the sucecss in this line was so great that, as the colony grew and increased, some individuals realising the fact that the country possessed unusual facilities for sheep-farming, imported some merino sheep from the mother country that were of Spanish origin; the result being that the wool obtained in Australia was found to be of actually finer quality than that grown upon the sheep fed upon the pastures of Spain!

From these humble beginnings has sprung up the enormous wool trade of Australia, the progress made by the first unthrifty race being so marked and satisfactory as to show to demonstration that the country was peculiarly well-fitted to carry sheep profitably, the first attempts at sheep-farming there turning out eminently sueeessful, and having now reached, as may be seen, very large proportions indeed.

Sheep inhabit a wide geographical range, and wild species are to be found in various parts of the world, the various races being generally divided by naturalists into five classes.

1st. The *ovis aries*, or domesticated sheep, including all the different varieties that have come under the care of the shepherd at various periods, and under widely different circumstances.

2nd. *Ovis argali*, or Asiatic sheep, which are found in the elevated plains of that continent, and in the Himalayan range.

3rd. *Ovis tragelaphus*, or bearded argali, whose general figure bears some resemblance to a deer, and are principally found in the mountainous parts of Egypt, and the inland districts of the Barbary States. It is worthy of remark here that these and similar races have caused some naturalists to hesitate in classing sheep as being generically distinct from the goat, for though a wide distinction exists between the woolly skin of one of our highly-bred domesticated long-woolled sheep and the hairy skin of the goat, yet the difference is not so marked and wide between a hairy-woolled sheep and the former. Wilson says, "The form and structure of the sheep, in its natural and unsubdued condition, differ in few material points from those of the goat. Even the skeletons of these two animals, when compared together, possess no points of difference which pass beyond the range of merely specific distinctions, and their digestive and other organs are equally conformable. We also know that hybrids or mixed breeds have been produced between the goat and the ewe, and between the ram and the she-goat, and it has been asserted that the male animals themselves were not, as usually happens, entirely unproductive; a fact which, if ascertained, would prove a closer mutual relationship to exist between the two species in question than that between the horse and the ass."

4th. *Ovis montana*, or Rocky Mountain sheep, which are found in the altitudes of the ranges of mountains in North America.

5th. *Ovis musmon*, which may be seen in our newly-acquired dependency, Cyprus, and the island of Crete, as well as in the mountains of Greece.

There are other wild species that are met with in some parts of Africa, and in other countries, that have been noticed by travellers; and it remains to this day an unsettled question, from which original race our domesticated species is to be traced.

There have been various speculations set afloat as to the time when sheep-farming was first cultivated in Britain, and, as at the time of its invasion by the Romans, coarse woollen fabrics of native manufacture abounded, it is surmised that the wool of which they were made must have been derived from domesticated flocks.

After the Romans had settled down in Britain, and manufactures began to be established, some of a comparatively rude nature, while others were more advanced, woollen goods took up a very prominent position amongst the crude manufactures of the day, for British woollen goods were sent to Rome, where they were prized for their extreme fineness.

Circumstances—such as the possession of coal—have caused the principal seats of textile manufacture to become established in the more northern portion of this kingdom; but it was not so during the earliest periods of English history, the southern counties being in this respect much more important than the northern ones, Winchester continuing for many centuries to be the head of the woollen trade, the extreme fineness of its woollen textures earning for it a deserved celebrity.

It may incidentally be remarked here, in corroboration of this fact in connection with early English industry in the southern counties, that Sussex iron was formerly very celebrated, one of the last mementoes of this branch of production being exhibited in the iron railings which used to surround St. Paul's Cathedral in London, which were cleared away and sold a few years back, and which were of Sussex manufacture.

To the growth of the woollen industry in Britain, which may be fairly regarded as an indigenous one, and the consequent demand for wool, may be traced the first efforts made for the improvement of the breed of sheep, which have gradually increased during the course of centuries, culminating in the efforts of Bakewell and the improvement of the breed known as the *Dishley breed;* the altered circumstances of late years necessitating the rearing of sheep for the *butcher,* rather than the *manufacturer* in the shape of wool, the finer fibre from our Australian and other colonies, fetching much higher prices than the coarser wool now grown upon English sheep, the carcases of which have been greatly improved by judicious

breeding, as well as weight of wool, though the quality must necessarily be coarser in accordance with the well-known result with
highly-fed animals which live in an artificial state, in contradis-
tinction to those which procure their sustenance from the spon-
taneous productions of the soil in the shape of natural grasses. The
wool of the small, short-woolled breeds that are fed upon hilly
pastures are superior in this respect to those animals of large
size ; but what has been lost in fineness of quality has been more
than made up for in length, and in the weight of the fleece; so that
now what are known as the *combing* wools predominate in England;
but in the times of which we have spoken, and this country depended mainly upon its own supply of sheep for wool, the description
known as *clothing* was principally aimed at by producers. At the
beginning of the tenth, and during the three following centuries—
although the value of a sheep and a pound of wool would seem
extremely small at the prices then current, taking into account the
great difference in the value of money, the worth of a wether was
computed at about 20s., and a pound of wool at 3s. 6d. to 3s. 9d., at
present values. In 1315, by a law that was enacted, no one was
permitted to demand more than 20d., equivalent to 25s. now, for a
fat sheep; but if it was shorn, the price was fixed at 14d., *i.e.*, 17s. 6d.
The average value of a fleece at this period was estimated at sixpence, or about 7s. 6d. in our present money, very nearly amounting
to half the value of the carcase. At the present time at which we
are writing, the rates for Kent wool in the Canterbury market are
extremely low, new fleeces being only 9d. to 10d. per lb.; lambs,
6d. to 7d.; old Kent fleeces, 8d. to 9d.; lambs, 6d. to 7d.

The characteristics of the sheep, more especially in a wild state,
are—a head furnished with triangular, spiral horns, larger in the
case of the male than that of the female, but altogether absent in
some of the highly-bred domesticated varieties, with two rudimen-
tary hooves on the fore legs situated on the inside, just above the
real toes ; two inguinal teats ; and the tail, always short in the wild
breeds, but varying in the domesticated species, some being very
long.   The fleece is of varying fineness and quality—depending
upon climate, food, and other circumstances. In the case of the
wild sheep, the external covering consists of long, coarse hair, beneath which is a coat of short, fine wool, while in the domesticated
species it consists of a fleece which varies in the different breeds,
to which we shall afterwards refer.   The mouth of the sheep is furnished with eight incisor teeth in the lower jaw, but none in the

upper, and six molars on either sides of both jaws, which makes a total of thirty-two. The sheep is a gregarious animal, both in its wild and domesticated state, assembling in flocks of greater or lesser numbers according to the circumstances of their condition, which vary extremely; each breed being marked by some peculiarity or other; and differing in size, flavour of the meat, quantity and quality of the wool, as aforesaid, as well as in hardihood, according to the nature of the soil and climate where they are bred; which causes the carcases of the small breeds which feed upon the thin-soiled uplands of the downs, and mountainous heathy pasture, to be covered with a thick coat of short, but fine wool; while those fed upon the marshes, and various rich low-lying bottoms, acquire larger frames, and longer and coarser wool; which circumstance has occasioned sheep in England to be classed under the two main divisions of *short-woolled* and *long-woolled sheep.* Some of these are polled, and some are horned, of which we shall proceed to give a detailed description.

3. **BREEDS AND VARIETIES.**—The only foreign sheep that have not been imported into Great Britain upon anything like an extended, and continuous scale for breeding purposes have been the Merino, which have been sent over at different times from Spain, where they are held in high estimation on account of the excellent quality of their wool; though in this country they have been proved, after many trials, to be unprofitable, and their cultivation as a regular breed has been almost entirely abandoned.

4. **THE MERINO SHEEP.** — Pure merinos are found both horned and polled, the weight of fleece in the yolk and unsmeared weighing 4 lbs. to 5 lbs., the dead weight of the flesh per quarter being from 15 to 18 lbs. The males have large spiral horns, of which the females are usually deficient, the face and legs being mostly white, though sometimes they are seen of a black or dun colour; a tuft of coarse wool is found on the forehead and cheeks; the nose and skin is commonly of a reddish flesh colour; the limbs long, the sides flat, and the chest narrow; to the eye of the experienced sheep-farmer presenting the appearance of an unprofitable breed, so far as the production of mutton is concerned, which is borne out by the facts; the race possessing only slow feeding powers. The looseness of skin under the throat, unsightly in the eyes of those accustomed to rest them upon more shapely forms, is said to be indicative of a fine fleece, which is indeed their only recommendation.

The changed conditions which now prevail, and to which we have before alluded in connection with the subject of colonial wool, have caused the keeping of sheep in England chiefly for the sake of their wool to be out of the question, for in the extensive plains of Australia, New Zealand and the Cape, immense flocks of fine-woolled sheep can be kept at a trifling expense, their wool being exported to England; so that all finer qualities of woollen

MERINO SHEEP.

fabrics are now made from Colonial wool; the sheep being more valuable in this island on account of his mutton than his fleece, the quality of the latter being consequently neglected for the former.

5. ENGLISH SHEEP.—The improvements of late years in the breeds of sheep have been very marked and conspicuous in the large breeds, especially the Leicesters, which have received an unusual degree of attention from various breeders, but more especially from Robert Bakewell; before referred to, of Dishley, near Lough-

borough, but there is little doubt that, if the like care and attention were taken to improve any particular breed, the same advantageous results might be obtained.

Sheep in Great Britain are classed under the following two main divisions of long-woolled and short-woolled varieties ; some of which are horned, and some polled.

LONG-WOOL.

Leicester and Lincoln .... polled.
Romney Marsh .... ,,
Bampton Notts .... ,,
South Ham .... ,,
Cotswold .... ,,
Dishley.. ,,
Teeswater .... ,,
Irish.. ,,

SHORT-WOOL.

Pure merino-horned............................ polled.
Southdown .... ,,
Wilts and Chiltern .... horned.
Dorset .... ,,
Portland .... ,,
Exmoor and Dartmoor .... ,,
Cornish .... ,,
Ryeland .... polled.
Dean Forest and Mendip .... horned.
Norfolk .... ,,
Cannock Heath.................................. polled.
Shropshire Morf .... horned.
Delamere Forest .... ,,
Herdwick.. polled.
Cheviot .... ,,
Scotch Heath.................................... horned.
Shetland......................................horned and polled.
Welsh Mountain .... ,,   ,,
Irish.. horned.

a. **LEICESTER SHEEP.**—The *new* Leicester sheep, as they were formerly termed, after the improvement made upon the *old* Leicester sheep by Bakewell, who first directed his attention to the matter about the year 1755, have become famous, and they are now sent all over the world for breeding purposes. The original stock was composed of large, awkward, large-boned animals, which did not arrive at maturity until they were three years old, being clothed with a long, coarse fleece, the weight of which would average about 10 lbs.

The weight of wool and size of the animals were great points in their favour ; but as they made fat but slowly, and consumed more food in proportion to their yield of meat, and more than the smaller breeds, these were very great drawbacks, and, to remedy them, Bakewell set to work.

His principal aim, as far as his system of procedure is known, appears to have been the improvement of the carcase, regarding the production of wool as of secondary importance; and in this respect they do not equal some of the breeds which they have displaced, being excelled in weight of fleece by the old Leicester, old Lincoln, and Romney Marsh sheep; the *average* weight of Leicester wool being 7 lbs. or 8 lbs., instead of 10 lbs., as formerly; though in exceptional instances shearling rams have been known to give a clip of 16 lbs. and 17 lbs.; and the Leicester sheep, as we now find

LEICESTER EWE.

it, may be said to belong more to the middle than long-woolled breeds; yet their general excellence have caused them to be adopted in most districts where the grass is rich and abundant, and they have pushed aside the old Lincolns, once a very favourite breed with flock-masters whose pasturage was of a suitable description to carry them; and Leicesters are now most commonly seen in the county of Lincoln and all the other neighbouring counties of Leicestershire.

The quality of the mutton of the Leicester sheep is considered to be superior to that of any other large breed, when not overfed, the fat and lean being more equally distributed, though the meat may not be relished so well by many, as the smaller breeds, as Welsh or Dartmoor mutton, and similar kinds, more suited to delicate palates; but in houses of business where a great number of hearty eaters are employed, and in most manufacturing districts where large mutton sells best, the Leicester is generally well appreciated, notwithstanding that the Leicester breed has never been a favourite one with the butcher, on account of its containing a small amount of offal, which it is customary to sink; but to the grower or feeder, whose object is weight of carcase, this would naturally be rather a recommendation than not.

The good points in the Leicester consist, in the first place, of the comparatively early age at which they may be fattened, and the short time it takes to effect the process; and next, the small quantity of food that is consumed, when placed against the weight of carcase attained: these united with the "fine handling," and the important fact that perhaps they will bring the greatest amount of profit to the feeder, are good and tangible reasons for the high estimation in which the breed is universally held.

On this account, the Leicester is employed very extensively all over the country for cross-breeding purposes, and even in the extreme north—where nothing but Cheviots were at one time to be seen, being considered the most appropriate breed for the district—crosses with the Leicester, by which the size of the frame of the original animal is very much increased, are now commonly met with The same also prevails in Wales, and other parts of the kingdom where the value of the breed has come to be appreciated.

The custom of letting out rams appears to have been unknown before the time of Bakewell, who, according to Youatt, commenced the practice about the year 1760; but he was so slenderly rewarded at the first beginning that, it is said, his first ram was let for the insignificant sum of 17s. 6d. But this, however, was not for long, for when the quality of his breed became known, the price of letting out his rams gradually rose, until, in the years 1784 and 1785, he was receiving as high as 100 guineas for the use of a ram; and they at last became so much in request that it is recorded he made 1,200 guineas in the year 1789 by three rams; and 2,000 guineas by seven others; the Dishley Society giving him 3,000 guineas for the use of the rest of his flock.

The same author states that the most extraordinary letting in the case of Bakewell's rams occurred in the instance of a ram named the "Two Pounder," for the use of which, during one season, he obtained 400 guineas each from two breeders; still reserving one-third of the usual number of ewes for himself; the value of the ram for that season being thus rated at 1,200 guineas.

Since the time of Bakewell, however, the appearance of the Lei-cester sheep has somewhat changed, for succeeding breeders, while acknowledging and appreciating the general excellence of his sheep, have grafted other qualities in which the Dishleys were deficient ; such as an increased quantity of wool, the improvement of the ewes so far as relates to better milking properties, and greater fecundity. These changes have depended often upon the taste, fancy, and opinions of various breeders in different counties, which has caused the breed to vary very much in its outward appearance in different districts; so that the wool of one set will be long and curly, while in another the fibre is closer and comparatively short ; in one district the animals wear a hardy, sprightly appearance ; in others an animal slower in its movements, and duller, being larger in size and bare-headed, is found|; yet all retaining, in a great measure, those ex-cellent qualities which in the first place earned the reputation of the original breed.   These have been described as having a small head covered with short white hair; an open countenance and clear muzzle; a full, quiet eye ; long, thin, but well-placed ear; a full, tapering neck, and deep, wide chest; uniformly broad and straight, firm back, terminating in a square rump, with full, deep shoulder, well-arched rib, and light offal; long, full quarter; well-turned hoist ; uniformly fine bone, with thin, soft, elastic pelt.

Writers who have referred to Bakewell's sheep nearer to the time when he was making his improvements in stock, give certain par-ticulars which it is interesting to note, on account of the changes that have taken place in the original breed.

The Complete Grazier; or, Farmer and Cattle Dealer's Assistant, published in 1805, written by "A Lincolnshire Grazier," contains at the commencement of the work a large folded sheet, in the shape of a map, which is styled "A Table of the breeds of Neat Cattle, Sheep, and Swine," the foot-note to which embodies the following:— " This table is selected, it is hoped, with some improvement from Mr. Culley's valuable 'Synopsis of Breeds,' annexed to his excellent work on Live Stock, such additions and variations being given from authentic sources, as the subject required."

The description given in this sheet of the Dishley, or New Leicester, is :—" Heads clean, straight, and broad ; bodies round or barrel-shaped ; eyes fine and lively ; bones fine and small ; pelts thin ; wool long and fine, well calculated for combing, and weighing upon on average eight pounds per fleece, when killed at two years old.   Fatten kindly and early, being admirably calculated for the market, thriving on pastures that will scarcely keep other sheep, and requiring less food than others. Tolerably hardy and vigorous."

The short space of time the Leicesters take in arriving at early maturity constitutes a very important feature in their value. Many flock-masters have them ready for the butcher when fifteen or sixteen months old, just after being shorn; while, with the exception of ewes and rams, none are kept after they are two years old; but in order to do this, it is necessary to keep them well and abundantly fed from the day they are dropped till they get into the hands of the butcher.

At the time of Bakewell and his immediate successors the Leicester ewes were less prolific than many other kinds, seldom producing twins, which, besides, was not thought desirable, the ewes not giving so much milk as other breeds; and being but indifferent nurses, one lamb was found quite enough to be brought up satisfactorily; even one lamb, at times, being reared with some little difficulty on the part of the mother. In most districts, in the case of other breeds of sheep, a moderate average of lambs dropped is considered to be when half the number of ewes in a flock produce twins, this proportion being often exceeded. And of late years there has been a marked improvement in this respect with Leicester ewes; and though not giving so much milk, nor being so prolific as many other breeds, yet they do not now show such a marked deficiency as formerly used to be the case.

Youatt, in speaking of the new Leicesters, says, that "on good keep they will yield a greater quantity of meat, for the same quantity of food, than any other breed of sheep can do. The kind of meat which they yield is of a peculiar character. When the sheep are not over fattened, it is tender and juicy, but, in the opinion of many persons, somewhat insipid. When they are raised to their highest state of condition, the muscles seem to be partially absorbed; at least much fatty matter is introduced between their fibres; the line of distinction between the fat and the lean is in a manner lost, and with the exception of a few joints, and a small part of them, the carcase has the appearance and the taste of a mass of luscious fat."

7. **FIVE-YEAR-OLD MUTTON.**—Of course it is of great advantage to the breeder to have profitable stock that becomes marketable at an early age, but in point of fact, mutton is not at its best till it is five years old, when it has attained a dark colour, and possesses a fine flavour; while in the case of a sheep of only two years old, the flesh will be of a pale colour, and comparatively insipid. This is well known to good judges of mutton, though not to the multitude.

The writer once had an amusing case pass beneath his notice, of a farmer who had a five-year-old sheep stolen from him. He accompanied a police-officer to the cottage of a man whom he suspected of stealing it, and upon the door being opened, their olfactory nerves were saluted by an unmistakable smell of roasting mutton. The farmer at once got excited, and cried out, " That's my sheep, I'll swear to it, *by the smell.*"

The police-officer, whose notions of evidence required a much more matter-of-fact groundwork to work upon, such as the skin of a sheep duly marked with certain signs that might be deposed to, or something of a tangible nature, was scandalised by such a hasty assumption of a man's guilt being arrived at through the bare *smell* of a cooking joint. Yet the farmer's belief was, to a certain extent, justified, and not so unreasonable as many might suppose ; for, added he, " I'll swear there's no such mutton as that about these parts, except mine." He was aware of the ordinary custom of disposing of stock at an early age, when the taste and smell of a mature sheep, the latter of which he recognised, could not be had.

8. **LINCOLN SHEEP.**—These, in their original state, are a large breed of sheep ; but their size has of late years been considerably diminished by crosses with the *new* or improved Leicester, as they were formerly called. The original Leicester, Lincoln, and Tees-water breeds, which were all noted for their large size, have been lessened considerably from their original proportions ; and it has been remarked that, before the period of which we are speaking, the mutton of these coarse sheep seldom amounted to more than half of their live weight. Judicious crossing has consider-ably decreased the quantity of offal, and added largely to the dead weight of marketable flesh, conferring smallness of bone and symmetry of form, whereas the common average, as recorded by experiment, will amount to more than two-thirds.

In the *Leicester Report*, two sheep bred from Dishley stock, with-out any unusual method of feeding, gave out the following results, the proportion of bone in a well-fattened animal being supposed to be an ounce, to one pound of flesh :—

Carcase............	144 lbs.	0 oz.		144 lbs.	6 oz.	
Fat..................	15 ,,	8 ,,		16 ,,	8 ,,	
Wool and Pelt...	16 ,,	0 ,,		18 ,,	0 ,,	
Pluck..............	4 ,,	8 ,,		8 ,,	8 ,,	
Entrails	10 ,,	4 ,,	.	3 ,,	8 ,,	
Blood..............	6 ,,	0 ,,		5 ,,	0 ,,	

In the improvement of original breeds, the trade of ram-letting attained great prominence, and considerable sums were paid for their use, which Marshall also refers to in his *Rural Economy of the Midland Counties*, the cost of the hire of tups, according to his account, prior to 1780, being from one guinea to ten for the season, recording the same facts as those before-mentioned by Youatt, as to the rise in Bakewell's stock, the price increasing from 10 to 100 guineas; from 178b to 1789 the prices rising so fast that 400 guineas were repeatedly given, several other breeders making from 500 to 1,000 guineas each.

An account is also given of the tup-masters of Leicestershire, in the *Leicester Report*, who formed themselves into a club, and bound themselves by certain rules and regulations which tended to keep up the value of the stock by which they profited so largely; breeders in various parts of the country imitating their example. And considering now the moderate rates that are paid for the hire of the best tups, it is often a matter of surprise how such large sums could ever have been realised; and this has been explained that it could only answer the purpose of speculators who counted upon the great profit to be obtained by letting their rams out, which was supported by the following calculation :—

If five persons have each twenty ewes good enough for ram-breeding, and pay 500 guineas for the hire of a tup, they have a good chance—reckoning twin lambs—of each rearing ten rams and ten ewes, or more, of a still higher blood. Now, supposing these ten ram-lambs, when shear-hogs, to be let out at twenty guineas each, upon the average, this would yield, upon the whole, 1,000 guineas, or cent. per cent. within two years; besides the future use of the rams, and the further improvement of the stock bred from the ewes. The preservation of the old breed of Lincoln sheep in its original form is now therefore seldom aimed at, and the bulk of the stock of what are now termed Lincolns, are merely the base or original of the old breed upon which has been grafted the new Leicester; for otherwise it would be manifestly a bad practice to overlook the improvement of stock that can be so easily effected by proper management.

9. SOUTHDOWN SHEEP.—This celebrated breed takes its name from the range of chalky hills in the county of Sussex, beginning at the east end and extending for sixty miles westward into Hampshire, which are termed the South Downs. This range is of an average breadth of about five miles, having a tract of arable land on either side, which is, cultivated by what are termed the Down farmers, the source of an abundant supply of artificial food for the sheep during the winter and spring months.

The natural pasturage of these hills is particularly well adapted for the feeding of sheep, being short and fine, while the elevation of the land and the dryness of the climate are peculiarly well-suited for keeping large numbers of sheep; and though there have not been, to our knowledge, any exact statistics of the numbers, Luccock, in his work *On Sheep*, estimated that not less than 864,000 were to be found on the Downs and the cultivated land of Sussex, and since that work was written the numbers have, doubtless, largely increased.

Of the early history, so to speak, of Southdown sheep, there does not appear to be any special or authentic records ; but it has been surmised that the elder races, in common with most breeds of hill-sheep, had horns, a male lamb being occasionally seen with small horns ; and it has been assumed that the original colour was mostly black, though few black Southdowns are now seen.   In Young's *Annals of Agriculture*, Mr. Alfrey says that—

" He is convinced that were the Southdown breed to be left in a wild state, they would in a few years become entirely black; for there are, every year, notwithstanding all the care that can be taken to prevent it, great numbers of black and white lambs, some with large black spots, some half black, and some entirely black; having had twelve and fourteen of the latter in a year, though he never kept a black lamb or ewe."

SOUTHDOWN EWE.

By the painstaking care of one individual, Mr. John Ellman, of Glynde, near Lewes, in Sussex, the race of Southdowns was considerably improved.   He describes the original breed as being formerly of small size, and far from possessing a good shape, being long and thin in the neck, high on the shoulders, low behind, high on the loins, down on the rump, the tail set on very low, almost perpendicularly from the hip-bones, sharp on the back, the ribs flat, not bowing, narrow in the fore-quarters, good in the leg, although having a large bone, the fleece being comparatively light, and not arriving at an age when they might be fattened advantageously till three years old.

Such was the original description of the Southdown stock, but under Ellman's care and attention they became so vastly improved as to be described by Arthur Young, in about the year 1794, as follows :—

" Mr. Ellman's flock of sheep, I must observe in this place, is unquestionably the first in the country ; there is nothing that can be compared with it; the wool the finest, and the carcase the best proportioned ; although I saw several of the noblest flocks afterwards, which I examined with a great degree of attention; some few had very fine wool, which might be equal to his, but then the carcase was ill-shaped, and many had a good carcase with coarse wool; but this incomparable farmer has eminently united both these characteristics in his flock at Glynde. I affirm this with the greater degree of certainty since the eye of prejudice has been at work in this county to disparage and call in question the quality of his flock, merely because he has raised the merit of it by unremitted attention above the rest of the neighbouring farmers, and it now stands unrivalled."

The original efforts of Ellman were afterwards supplemented by the Duke of Richmond, Mr. Jonas Webb and others, and continued improvement of the herd carried on, the points in which they were deficient being supplied by careful crossing, so that they are now fully equal to any of the best breeds in the kingdom, attaining to maturity early, and having altered very much from their original description . as described by Mr. Ellman, being smaller in the bone, possessing a greater aptitude to fatten, combined with a heavier carcase when fat, and yet being equally hardy.

Southdown sheep now come regularly round, fit for the butcher, at from fifteen months to two years old; the dead weight per quarter averaging 18 to 20 lbs., though in exceptional cases they weigh much heavier; from 12 to 14 lbs. being formerly usually considered a fair weight for a Down wether two years old.

This must be considered a great weight for a breed like the Southdown, which partakes of the nature of a race that feeds on mountainous districts with comparatively short herbage; while the weight of the fleece of the old Down has been nearly doubled, the meat always being held in the highest estimation, and often fetching from a halfpenny to a penny a pound more in the market than many other kinds.

When we speak of the Down sheep partaking somewhat of the nature of mountain sheep, it must be pointed out that there is a difference between what are termed the hill and the lowland grazing sheep. Originally the wool of the former weighed but 2 lbs. or so, latterly increased to 3½ lbs.; and from 4 lbs. it has risen to 6 lbs. in the case of the latter.

In all the southern parts of the kingdom, the Southdown is found to answer remarkably well, and the race is pushing aside the sheep indigenous to other counties, the old Berkshire being now very rarely seen, while in Hampshire the old breed peculiar to that county is not often met with. Even Norfolk and Suffolk, which at one time boasted of breeds of special excellence. when compared with some of the old, inferior breeds, have been crossed with Southdown and Leicester sheep; a cross between a Southdown and almost every breed of middle-wool sheep being found to answer extremely well.

At one time the large, coarser black-faced sheep, often termed Southdowns, but technically known as West Couutry Downs, which were sent from Dorsetshire and Somersetshire, are being displaced by the pure Downs even in their native *habitat.*

Culley, in describing the Southdown sheep in 1807, remarks that: " These sheep stand higher behind than before, and the hind-quarters are generally heavier than the fore-quarters, which in Sussex (the district they are bred in) is esteemed a merit, as the butchers sell the former at fully one penny per lb. more than the latter—a singularity that we believe is peculiar to this district; for, in all the other markets we have seen, the hind-quarters, and particularly the legs, are sold for a halfpenny per lb. less than the fore-quarters. This breed of sheep being hardy and ready feeders, we hope the defect will be remedied in a few years, and other improvements made by the attention and exertion of enterprising breeders, particularly the ingenious Mr. Ellman, of Glynde, whose flock is already superior to most of his neighbours, both in carcase, quantity, and quality of wool."

It will be seen from this description that the fact of the hinder quarters being heavier than the fore-quarters is regarded as a defect, though legs of mutton fetch a penny *more,* instead of less, than shoulders in the London market. This, though doubtless in the eye of the breeder, in the general symmetry and *tout ensemble* of an animal, would be termed a *defect,* in the eye of the London butcher certainly would not stand for one.

10. **WEIGHTS PER QUARTER OF DIFFERENT BREEDS.**— The following table will show at a glance about the average weight per quarter of the different breeds of sheep, which it must be understood are greatly exceeded at times in individual instances:—

	Dead weight of the flesh per quarter.		Dead weight of the flesh per quarter.
Pure Merino	18 to 20 lbs.	Shropshire Morf	9 to 13 lbs.
Leicester and Lincoln	24 to 32 „	Delamere Forest	8 to 10 „
Teeswater	26 to 36 „	Herdwick	9 to 12 „
South Down	18 to 22 „	Cheviot	12 to 18 „
Wilts	14 to 18 „	Scotch Heath	13 to 16 „
Dorset	16 to 20 „	Shetland	8 to 9 „
Portland	8 to 10 „	Welsh Mountain	9 to 11 „
Dartmoor	10 to 12 „	Irish (horned)	10 to 14 „
Cornish	12 to 15 „	Bampton Notts	22 to 28 „
Ryeland	13 to 16 „	South Ham	18 to 22 „
Dean Forest	12 to 14 „	Cotswold	26 to 34 „
Norfolk	14 to 18 „	Dishley	21 to 25 „
Cannock Heath	16 to 20 „	Irish (polled)	22 to 26 „

LEICESTER RAM.

CHAPTER II.

BREEDS AND VARIETIES OF SHEEP (continued).

The Dorset—House Lamb—The Ryeland—Cheviot Sheep—Black-faced or Heath breed of Sheep—The Romney Marsh Sheep—The Teeswater—The Herdwick—The Cotswold—The Bampton Long-wools—Irish Sheep—Welsh Sheep—Exmoor and Dartmoor Sheep—Orkney and Shetland Sheep.

11. **THE DORSET.**—The Dorset sheep are possessed of a peculiar distinction as respects their fecundity, being remarkable as good nurses, and for receiving the male much earlier in the season than any other race of English sheep, taking the ram in May and June, so that their lambs are dropped in October and November.

12. **HOUSE LAMB.**—This fact has caused them to be celebrated as "house lamb," which is sold as a delicacy in the London market about Christmas-time, and during the course of January, when it fetches a high price, some of the farmers who live in the counties abutting upon the metropolis purchasing ewes that are in lamb with the view of fattening the latter first, and the last afterwards; the earliest lambs, which are slaughtered just before Christmas, being most of them bred in the house with a good deal of attention and care, which all farmers are not willing to undertake.

The ewes selected by those who turn their attention to suckling lambs are chosen of large size, and preferred with white noses, anything like black on the nose being considered objectionable. The colour of the flesh of the lambs when butchered is another point of significant importance, as it considerably affects their value, and therefore those that can be warranted to *die fair* always command the highest price. As this warranty could not be given when ewes are promiscuously bought at a fair, the breeders with whom the *sucklers*, as they are called, deal, are obliged to be careful in the selection of rams, so as to ensure white meat in the progeny; and this result, it is said, can be foretold by certain marks in the mouth.

This fact is remarked both in the *Middlesex* and *Hertfordshire Reports*, the former stating that "the sucklers, salesmen, and butchers of London are aware that such lambs as have sharp barbs on the inside of their lips, are certainly of a deep colour after being butchered, and all those whose *barbs are naturally blunt*, do as certainly produce fair meat; the issue of such rams can also be generally warranted fair." In the *Hertfordshire Report* the description is, *those with white barbs*.

The Dorset is generally considered one of the best of the short-woolled, horned breeds, and may be met with in their original purity in some parts of Dorsetshire; but it is customary to put the old ewes which are intended to be sold, to the Southdown ram, the lambs being found to thrive faster, and, being free from horns, and having dark faces, are on these accounts preferred.

Both ewes and rams have horns of small size, wearing a tuft of wool on the forehead, the face being long and broad, and, as well as the head, white. The hind-quarters are good, but the fore ones are somewhat deficient, the loin being broad and deep, which is generally regarded as being indicative of superior milking qualities. The bone is by no means large, though they stand high upon their limbs; but the wool is only of medium quality, and not over-abundant, weighing about 4 lbs. per fleece. They are excellent sheep for folding; contented upon a somewhat short allowance of food, being hardy and active, and capital travellers; amply evidenced by the fact that ewes in lamb are sometimes driven fifty, or even sixty miles to Weyhill fair, one of the largest sheep fairs in the kingdom, the journey occupying about a week, which they bear remarkably well.

13. **THE RYELAND.**—The Ryeland takes its name from a tract of sandy land in Herefordshire on the borders of Wales, which was once celebrated for its growth of rye—and hence the term "Ryeland"—where they have existed as a distinct breed for many centuries, being one of the most distinctive of the old upland races.

It is a small but compact animal, of symmetrical proportions, fattening readily; the fat itself accumulating internally more than upon the external muscles; which is considered to make the best mutton. Both the rams and ewes are polled, the colour of the face, legs and fleece being white, and having a tuft of wool on the forehead. The limbs are short, the loin being very broad and full. At one time the wool of the Ryeland sheep fetched a high price, but, as before pointed out, the importation of colonial wool into England of late years has produced quite a revolution in the management of sheep, so far as their growth for the production of wool is concerned.

When this consideration was uppermost, it was thought that, by crossing them with the Spanish merino, the already fine quality of the fleece would become yet further improved; but experience proved these expectations to be ill-founded, and the Ryeland turned out to be less susceptible of improvement and amalgamation with different races than any other breed of English sheep.

The numbers of Ryeland sheep have been greatly diminished of late years; it having been estimated that Herefordshire alone contained half-a-million of short-woolled sheep in the year 1800, which produced 4,200 packs of wool, the weight of each fleece being but 2 lbs.

Although the Ryeland is a breed that is much liked by those who are used to them, many flockmasters have reluctantly given them up in favour of a more profitable race of animals.

14. CHEVIOT SHEEP.—The range of hills termed the Cheviots, which divide Northumberland from Scotland, are separated from one another by valleys, which, from time immemorial, have been celebrated for producing a breed of sheep comparatively large of carcase, and good yield of wool, combined with great hardiness, which causes them to be an extremely valuable breed for the district.

The face and legs are white, except in the case of a few examples, in which these are mottled grey, which denotes peculiar hardiness, the head being erect, long, and clean, with neck and throat covered with wool, but, in the pure breed, with no wool on the head. The hind-quarters are full and well-proportioned, with full rumps; but there is a tendency to lightness in the fore-quarters. The fleece generally weighs from three to four pounds, the pelt being thin, and uniformly covered with fine wool, and free from dead hairs.

From the proximity of this range of hills to the sea (though the term Cheviot, strictly speaking, only applies to the highest hill, which is over 2,600 feet high, and is surrounded by other hills of lesser elevation) the loose snow in the winter season is often thawed to a considerable extent by the saline influence of the sea breezes. This thaw being frequently followed by frost, at times gives a surface of ice, which causes the sheep to obtain their food only with great difficulty, for patches of snow may be seen lying in the hollows up to midsummer. Owing, however, to the steep nature of the ground, the animals manage to scrape the obstacles away with their feet, and they are rarely fed with anything more than a little hay of a coarse kind, that is made in the district every year, the bulk of their food being derived from the pastures, which are steep, and hence dry; producing some excellent grasses, that are specially well suited for feeding sheep.

The character of Cheviot sheep has altered a good deal of late years, the attention of breeders having been effectually turned to its improvement; and many farmers of Northumberland have crossed them with Leicesters, fattening the breed so produced upon turnips and the richer pastures of their lowland farms.

In many cases the breed has been improved without the admixture of any foreign blood at all, by careful selection, and improvement of those qualities in which they were deficient—the Cheviot being naturally a good subject to work upon, the points, in all breeds, which constitute a good sheep being substantially the same. This course of procedure was found to answer better in the hilly districts than crossing with Leicester sheep, whose powers of assimilation, and adaptability to pastures situated in a high altitude, were at one time much over-rated—it being found that the coarse and scanty pasturage, in severe seasons, was inadequate to the support of such large-bodied sheep as the Leicesters and similar breeds. The lambs produced, as well, being unable to stand the effects of severe storms in elevated districts, the flocks suffered considerably in consequence.

Still, by a wise and judicious selection, in crossing a first-class Cheviot ewe with a ram that has a fair share of Leicester blood in him, originally descended from a cross between a Cheviot and a Leicester, a larger carcase has been obtained, with a quicker disposition to fatten, combined with the hardy properties of the pure Cheviot.

The geographical aspect of these mountain grazings has much to do with developing the physical, or bodily features of the race of animals placed upon them, which needs any alterations in their general characteristics to be made with skill and caution. And in

making changes, it is necessary not to have stock that will de-
teriorate when placed in its new quarters; there being many lofty
grazings, which, though too high to support a Leicester sheep,
would adequately maintain a larger animal than the pure Cheviot;
and this has been obtained for suitable districts, as before stated,
by crossing a Cheviot ewe with a Leicester ram. These, in some
districts, have been found to answer so well, that some farmers
keep what they call a pure half-bred stock—the produce of the first
cross between the Leicester ram and Cheviot ewe; these unite the
hardihood of one parent with the adaptability to fatten early of the
other, and when at two years, are found to have attained great
weights, comparatively.

The Cheviot sheep have been introduced into the Scottish Highlands, and have been found of great advantage to put upon the
lower pastures, upon which the comparatively inferior heath-sheep
were exclusively located at one time, which are contented, and thrive
upon the barren heights of mountainous districts, where no other
description of stock could be maintained, either successfully or
profitably.

At times, however, sufficient judgment has not been used in thus making
endeavours to secure a more profitable breed of animals, for some breeders,
whose poor land is only calculated for the support of heath, or black-faced
sheep, their pastures being stony and barren, have got in their place a breed of
small unthrifty Cheviots, when the heath-sheep would have answered their
purpose considerably better.

As the Cheviot breed very readily adapts itself to a great variety of climate, it
has been a matter of surprise that in Ireland and Wales, where there are extensive mountainous districts, the Cheviot breed of sheep has not been more
largely adopted than it has hitherto been.

15. **BLACK-FACED, OR HEATH BREED OF SHEEP.**—There
have been many conjectures as to the origin of the Black-faced, or
Heath breed of sheep, of the North of England and Highlands of
Scotland. A dim tradition exists that they were brought from
abroad by an early Scottish king; but it has been considered most
likely that they originated in the mountainous districts of the
northern counties of England, from whence they were introduced
into Scotland at an early date, where they have gradually spread
themselves, until they have become the prevailing breed in the
Highlands, in many districts subsisting upon herbage of the poorest
description, that would prove quite inadequate to the support of
any other breed.

The wool of most descriptions of mountain sheep is short and
fine, and thickly set, but the fleece of the black-faced sheep is long,

thin, and coarse, partaking of a hairy nature. A similar characteristic marks the alpaca, or bright-haired wool species, only the wool
of the alpaca is of immeasurably superior quality. The wool of the
heath breed is used in the manufacture of the most inferior and
coarse fabrics, the poorer kinds of wool being sometimes sold at so
low a rate as 4d. per lb.—the kind, technically known as "laid";
white in the same ratio fetching 5½d. per lb.; but in all probability
with greater care, and better housing and feeding, the quality of
the wool of the black-faced sheep might be greatly improved; but,
because the breed is a hardy one, they are left without those
mitigating contrivances and appliances that might be furnished,

HEATH EWE.

being often left unprotected from the effects of the bitter weather,
and prevailing snow-storms—the snow-drifts of winter, and the cold
rains of spring and autumn.

Sheep-houses have certainly been tried, in some parts, and have
been found not to answer, on account of the animals preferring to
remain in them, and getting half-starved, rather than face the
bitter blasts that sweep over some of these mountainous regions.
Clumps of plantations might with advantage be adopted in many
bare and exposed situations, that would break the force of the wind,
and afford shelter; while it has been pointed out that stone stalls,
of proper construction, might be placed in convenient situations,
that would mitigate the evils referred to, though they would be
inferior to plantations of Scotch firs, which would also bring in a
profit to the planters.

Notwithstanding the comparative neglect with which they are
often treated after the severest winters, when the lambing season
comes round they are invariably found to be in better condition
than any other breed of sheep that have to support life under
similar circumstances; though, doubtless, if they were furnished
with plenty of food at all times, and not allowed to shift so much
for themselves, they would attain to greater weights on their native
pastures.

In the pure breed, the carcase is long, round, and firm; the chest
wide, with full ribs and shoulders, and robust limbs; the face and
legs of the ram being black, or mottled; with a round tuft of softer
wool between the horns, the muzzle and lips being of the same light
shade of colour. The eye is lively and fiery, the ears moderately
long, with horns springing easily from the head, and inclining down-
ward and forward.

In the instance of the ewe, the horns are smaller, and not spirally
twisted, as is the case with the ram. The lambs are dropped two
or three days sooner than most breeds, and when born have horns
from one to two inches long, covered thinly with hair; and, when
intended to be kept as wedders, they are not castrated till they are
eight or ten weeks old, in order that the horns may not turn in too
suddenly, and injure their eyes. In districts that are not too much
exposed, the ewes generally have their first lambs when two years
old, but upon highly-situated farms, exposed to stormy weather,
they are not allowed to have lambs till they are three years old.
They are excellent nurses, and have, on this account, been made
use of for rearing fat lambs upon arable farms, when, having fed
their lambs, they are sold off.

16. **THE ROMNEY MARSH SHEEP.**—The Romney Marsh and
its neighbouring low-lying districts abutting the southern shores of
Kent and Sussex, have long been famous for a long-woolled breed of
sheep, the fleece finding a ready sale in Canterbury market, the
race being exceedingly well suited to the marsh land which lies
exposed to the rough gales of the Channel. Crosses of the Leicester
breed have also been largely used, which has improved their
bodily shape, without to any known extent impairing their hardihood, the original breed being characterised by thickness, and length
of head; long and thick neck and carcase; wide loin, large belly;
narrow fore-quarter; large bone; long and coarse wool.

The ewes are not supplied with hay during the winter, and have
in snowy weather to scrape the snow away with their feet; and,

during severe seasons, often become in very poor condition by lamb-ing time, the number of lambs reared being generally estimated to be about the same as the number of ewes that are put to ram; for although a higher average than usual of twins is born, a good many lambs are lost every year.

The lambs are weaned the first and second week in August; and are then often put out to be kept on upland farms, till about the first week in April; when they are getting in readiness for the spring grass in the Weald and greater portion of the county of Kent. As Romney Marsh and adjoining marshes contain something like 80,000 acres, great numbers of sheep are reared and fattened annually, the general system of management that is pursued by graziers being

ROMNEY MARSH EWE.

to keep a portion of the land for breeding, and a portion for fatten-ing stock. The breeding land is stocked with ewes in the autumn for the winter, at the rate of two and a half to three and a half, and sometimes as much as four sheep per acre; the rams being usually put to the ewes from the 12th to the 16th of November.

17. **THE TEESWATER.**—The old Teeswater was a large coarse-boned clumsy animal, with a wide back, and round barrel; a slow feeder and taking a long time to attain maturity, the wool being long and coarse, and thinly set; their *habitat* being the lowland districts on the borders of Durham and Yorkshire, their origin being, in all probability, the same as the old Lincolns, both of which breeds may now be said to have been improved away, the old fashioned Lincoln sheep being now seldom met with, except occa-

sionally in the rich marshes near the sea; which, according to Parkinson, was capable of carrying four fatting sheep per acre in summer, and two in winter.

One great recommendation possessed by the Teeswater is its prolific nature, twins not only being usual, but cases happening of as many as four, and even five lambs being produced at a birth by one ewe.

The old Teeswater have, however, been merged to a great extent in the Leicester, the cross having quickened their feeding properties, but reduced their size, and improved their wool.

18. **THE HERDWICK.**—An interesting account is given of the origin of the breed known as the Herdwick, which are the most valuable kind of mountain sheep to be found in the county of Cumberland. They are said to have descended from a few Scottish sheep that were saved from a vessel that was wrecked off the coast of Cumberland, and are reputed to shelter themselves instinctively from an approaching storm, and are remarkable for their activity in scraping away the snow that covers their pasturage in winter, as well as being celebrated for their great hardiness.

19. **THE COTSWOLD.**—The Cotswold are found in a large part of Gloucestershire, Oxfordshire, Herefordshire, Worcestershire, and the lowland districts of South Wales; and are supposed to take their name from the cots, or sheds, in which they were fed in the winter; and from the wolds, or open hilly grounds on which they fed in summer; being a heavier sheep than the Leicesters, but more active, with greater powers of endurance in supporting both hunger and cold.

It is considered one of the oldest breeds in the kingdom, the price of the wool per lb. of the Cotswold sheep, being distinctly mentioned in the year 1341, when it was reckoned to be worth four shillings of our present money. A present of Cotswold rams was made by Henry IV. to Henry of Castile, in 1469, and with the view of improving the Spanish long-woolled breed, John of Aragon received a similar present in 1468.

They are a fine race of animals, with large frames, ribs well springing out from back and chine, full hind-quarters and good thighs, with full and prominent chests, but at times found somewhat defective in depth from chine to chest. Their wool does not rank so high in value as many others, which excel it in length and weight; but they are a fine class of animals, held by many highly in favour, under the common appellation of "Gloucester" sheep, being peculiarly well fitted as stock for pastures that are exposed to cold and wet, and the damp mists that often overspread the Cotswold Hills. This breed has also received a considerable addition of Leicester blood, that is to say, the *new* Leicester blood; for, according to the description given by Marshall of the *old* Leicester, the portrait he draws is not at all an attractive one : describing them as having "a frame large and remarkably loose; his bone heavy, his legs long and thick, terminating in great splaw feet; his chine, as well as his rump, sharp as a hatchet; his skin rattling on his ribs, and his handle resembling that of a skeleton wrapped in parchment." Such is the description of the old Leicester sheep, given by an accurate writer of the day, so far as agricultural knowledge then extended; the shortcomings of which, however, had nothing to do with mere description of an animal as it then existed. With these unpromising materials to work with, an opinion may be justly formed of the value of Bakewell's labours, which, supplemented by the further exertions of others, has placed the Leicester breed of sheep upon the eminent position it now occupies.

20. **THE BAMPTON LONG-WOOLS.**—This breed of sheep takes its name from a village called Bampton, situated between Somerset-shire and Devonshire; standing on the borders of the two counties, where they were supposed to have been first bred. They are, how-ever, now found on nearly all the lower and best pasture-lands of North Devon, extending to the Vale of Taunton, and far into Somersetshire. But these have also been very extensively crossed by the Leicestershire breed; and they now bear a very close affinity to it, furnishing another proof of how widely the influence of one man's exertions—or it may be described as the intelligent manage-ment of one man, who first began a series of improvements, which other men followed up—may be made to spread over a whole kingdom.

Unfortunately the memory of Bakewell is tainted by the syste-matic selfishness he practised; for it is well known he had upon his estate some water-meadows, which being flooded early in the season, so as to bring a fresh growth of grass in the autumn, he put his superfluous stock upon them. Their improvement at first was very rapid, but they soon became tainted by rot—his practised eye at once detecting its early symptoms. They were then sold off without delay, being thus made unfit for breeding purposes—the chief end he had in view. But these and similar tactics were not adopted by Ellman, the great improver of the Southdowns, who was always happy to communicate his knowledge to others for their benefit.

21. **IRISH SHEEP.**— In Ireland there may be said to be two distinct breeds of sheep: a favourite breed of short-woolled sheep, that is commonly found in the county of Wicklow, and the original large Irish sheep, which, however, has become vastly improved of late years, and takes rank with some of the best English breeds.

The sheep of the Kerry and Wicklow hills possess distinctive features as a mountain breed, the Wicklow breed resembling Welsh sheep very much, with white faces and legs polled, and wild in their nature.

On the farms situated at the top of the mountains, or rather, perhaps, to which the top grazing grounds belong, on which the sheep are kept, they are of small size, increasing in bulk as they approach the base of the mountains. At their summits, the pasturage being scanty, and the ground generally very boggy, the sheep are often small, and the wool partakes of that hairy nature which has been described in the case of the black-faced sheep of the North of England, and Scotland—the fleece being less fine, and the hair showing itself in ridges about the spine and neck. This is a wise provision of Nature to counteract the evils of their position, which is also strikingly exemplified in the case of the lambs, which have a hairy covering on those parts of the frame which come in contact with the damp ground.

In Ireland, the Wicklow sheep, from the proximity of the district to Dublin, stands in much the same relationship as does the Dorset breed in England; the country farmers near the Irish metropolis buying up the ewes for the purpose of rearing house-lamb, contriving to have the lambs dropped in December, when they are allowed to remain with their mothers for about a fortnight, and are afterwards forced on by cow's milk, being crammed as much as possible, so as to be ready for the butcher at about six weeks old. The small size, however, of the Wicklow sheep is causing its numbers to be gradually lessened in favour of animals with larger frames, despite the good qualities it possesses.

The Kerry sheep are larger than the Wicklow breed, and may be regarded as the type of the natural mountain breeds of the West of Ireland, being larger also than the Welsh mountain sheep. They are wild and unthrifty, and take a long time to arrive at maturity; and are somewhat hard to fatten, which is generally the case with animals of a more than ordinarily lively nature; but when this has been done, they are liked very much, the mutton being considered of superior quality, though they cannot be regarded as a profitable race of sheep.

They are liked by the butcher, as they cut up better than their outward appearance would appear to indicate, and they contain a large proportion of loose fat.

22. **WELSH SHEEP.**—Welsh sheep indigenous to the mountains of the Principality are of small size, both ewes and rams

WELSH SHEEP.

being horned, with black noses, long necks, and fore-quarter low in proportion to the hind-quarters, having flat ribs and narrow chests; the wool on the sides being short and fine, and a ridge of coarse hair, the same as described in the case of the Wicklow sheep, extending from the neck to the tail, the throat as well being hairy. The fleece is proportionately small in volume, weighing only from one to two pounds; while the colours vary in all the different degrees of shade from white to black.

The mutton is highly esteemed for its delicate flavour, which suits a fastidious appetite much better than the larger breeds of sheep which abound in luscious fat; and considering the rarity of really good mutton being procurable—that is, mature mutton—which has before been described as not being at its best till five years old, Welsh mutton certainly forms a good substitute for first-class English mutton, which very few people taste now-a-days. As a rule, however, they are much neglected by London butchers, and are mostly sold by provision-dealers as an article of speciality in London, where the meat is procurable at very moderate rates, a venture generally being made in it when the season comes round for "hanging"—these remarks applying to the wilder race.

Another breed is the white-nosed, or soft-woolled; terms used to distinguish it from the former, which, although resembling the wilder race in restlessness of disposition, are different in other particulars, the females being rarely horned, though the males are so, the universal colour of the face and fleece being white; though there is a natural tendency to produce black rams, as if an old strain was continually asserting its presence. The largest sheep in the Principality are found in Anglesea, where there is better keep than on the Welsh hills, and the wool of the sheep in Wales is largely employed in making flannels, Newtown being the principal manufacturing centre. Welsh flannel is celebrated for its quality, which doubtless owes its excellence to the yolk, or grease, which the fleece of the Welsh sheep naturally possesses, which is found so efficacious in all cases of rheumatism.

As a rule, Welsh farming is much below the average, and there has not been that attention bestowed upon the matter which its importance deserves, with regard to the breeding of sheep.

23. **EXMOOR AND DARTMOOR SHEEP.**—Exmoor and Dartmoor sheep, generally, are considered to be the representatives of the old forest breeds of English sheep.

At one time they were divided into distinct classes, but they are gradually disappearing, and making way for the more profitable races. Originally the denizens of forests, subsisting in the open glades, the true forest sheep were small in size, and defective in bodily form, as sheep now are looked upon with the breeder's eye; though admirably adapted by the Wise Creator to pick up their living where it was to be found, being naturally wild, restless, and difficult to fatten, partaking more in their nature of the wild beasts of the forest, perhaps, than of the usually regarded tame and domesticated sheep, accustomed to the voice of the shepherd.

The faces and legs of the old forest sheep were of a russet brown, dun, or grey colour, though sometimes white, both ewes and rams being horned, and the fleece small in weight, often not exceeding two pounds.

24. **ORKNEY AND SHETLAND SHEEP.** — The sheep of the Orkney and Shetland islands are extremely hardy, and somewhat peculiar in their general characteristics, the fleece varying very much in colour, some being white or black, while others are pied or grey, the latter being much esteemed for making Shetland shawls,

EXMOOR RAM.

veils, and hosiery. An outer coat of hair, called by the natives of the islands "scudda," grows through the wool, which is not shorn, as is the case with other sheep, but is pulled off by the hand at the proper time ; for if left to itself it becomes detached at the beginning of summer, and falls off, leaving the hair before described as a covering.

This hair throws off the wet, and is a good defence against cold, the wool yielded by each sheep weighing about a pound and a half to two pounds, when thus obtained, but is found to be deficient of the felting properties which mark other kinds of wool.

They are hardy animals, capable of enduring severe weather, and of sustaining hunger ; and it is said of them that, during the winter months, they subsist to a very great extent upon *sea-weed*, possessing the remarkable instinct of distinguishing between the ebbing and flowing of the tide; upon its first ebbing, being seen to run down from the hills to the sea-shore in order to obtain it.

They are of small size, and vary considerably in weight, being generally polled, though many have small horns which are not spiral, but resemble those of the goat, more than the ordinary sheep. The tail is short and unusually broad, which is a distinguishing trait of the Scandinavian races, and they are altogether a hardy breed, capable of enduring the furious storms which rage at times in these northern islands.

The breeds of sheep we have named, embrace all the varieties that it is necessary to refer to, for any practical purpose, including as it does a list of all the best ones that are suitable for every possible situation and soil, from the barren heights of mountainous districts, to the rich grazings of lowland pastures, and marsh land. In each particular district there will be found breeds more in favour than others, which thus become, as it were, peculiar to every county, though, as will have been seen, the original breeds have often been displaced by more profitable stock, in many instances obtained by judicious crossing.

SOUTHDOWN RAM.

CHAPTER III.

PRELIMINARY MANAGEMENT.

How to Judge of Sheep—Uses of the Sheep—As Food—Wool—Preliminary Management of Sheep—Descriptive Names of Sheep at Different Ages—For ascertaining the Age of Sheep—Clay-land Farmers, and Turnip Husbandry.

25. **HOW TO JUDGE OF SHEEP.**—The reader will perceive, from what has been pointed out before, that the breeder, or grazier, should carefully acquaint himself with the nature of his land, and the resources at his command for feeding his animals, and then adopt the most likely breed of sheep that he considers best suited to his own particular circumstances and condition; but one salient point should always be held in remembrance—that no stock will succeed that is brought from a rich soil to an inferior one, for if so, they will inevitably decrease in value and condition; but the reverse will be the case if they come from off poorer land, when they will soon get in thriving order.

This principle is very apparent in the case of the small Scotch beasts and Highland cattle that are frequently bought to eat up the grass in gentlemen's parks. This, often somewhat poor in quality, though plentiful, sufficiently sustains the hardy race of animals that are put upon it, and they will get fat, when some of the large heavy breeds of cattle would be half-starved, and sensibly go back in condition; the feed, such as it is, being better than the coarse and scanty herbage to which the first are naturally accustomed; and the same applies equally to sheep.

Upon the quality of the food depends a good deal the forward or backward condition of the flock with respect to breeding, ewes

D

generally breeding at the age of fifteen or eighteen months, though many graziers will not admit the ram until they have attained two years of age. In judging of sheep, there are various points which recommend themselves to the breeders', or stock-keepers' attention; the choice of a ram having been aptly described by Culley as follows, a description that has often been quoted :—

" His head should be fine and small; his nostrils wide and expanded; his eyes prominent, and rather bold and daring; ears thin; his collar fuller from his breast and shoulders, but tapering gradually all the way to where the neck and head join, which should be very fine and graceful, being perfectly free from any coarse leather hanging down; the shoulders broad and full, which must at the same time join so easy to the collar forward and chine backward, as to leave not the least hollow in either place; the mutton upon his arm, or fore-thigh, must come quite to the knee; his legs upright, with a clean, fine bone, being equally clear from superfluous skin and coarse, hairy wool, from the knee and hough downwards; the breast broad and well forward, which will keep his fore-legs at a proper wideness; his girth, or chest, full and deep, and instead of a hollow behind the shoulders, that part, by some called the fore-flank, should be quite full; the back and loins broad, flat, and straight, from which the ribs must rise with a fine circular arch; his belly straight; the quarters long and full, with the mutton quite down to the hough, which should neither stand in nor out; his *twist* (*i.e.*, the junction of the inside of the thighs), deep; wide, and full; which, with the broad breast, will keep his four legs open and upright; the whole body covered with a thin pelt, and that with fine, bright, soft wool."

This description by Mr. Culley fully describes excellence of form in the ram; and the ewe requires also to be chosen with due discrimination when bought or selected for breeding purposes; a main point being that she is perfectly sound, as a matter of course, and this is indicated by the teeth being white, the gums red, the breath sweet and not fetid, the eyes lively, the feet cool, and the wool firm. These qualities, or the absence of them, will pretty clearly indicate health or incipient disease. In crossing sheep of different breeds, the general result that is aimed at must often of necessity differ a good deal, but there is a saying recorded of Sir John Sinclair, that a sheep would be brought to perfection were it possible to unite in the same animal the fleece of the Spanish merino, the carcase of the Bakewell, and the constitution of the Southdown. Experience has, however, shown that it is quite possible to breed for any particular quality that may be considered most desirable, and by proper care and attention in this way the owner of stock may supplement points in which his flock may be naturally deficient to a very material extent.

26. **USES OF THE SHEEP.**—As before remarked, the two main points to be considered in relation to the profit to be obtained from keeping sheep are the wool and mutton.

27. AS FOOD.—As food, the peculiarities of each leading breed as concerns the production of mutton, has been described; but this of late years has become of infinitely more importance than the growth of wool in England. Though the latter forms no inconsiderable portion of a farmer's profits, yet it has become a secondary consideration from the state or condition of affairs that now prevails, though it was not always so.

28. WOOL.—The wonderful impetus given to sheep-farming in

SHEARLING HAMPSHIRE DOWN RAM.

Australia, New Zealand, the Cape, and our other colonial possessions, has produced a thorough revolution in the comparative value of English wool for manufacturing purposes, which has caused the finest woolled sheep of the United Kingdom to be of far less account than formerly, in the production of wool.

Before this time, wool used to form one of the most profitable items in the returns from the flock, but now British wool is no longer sought for in the production of fine woollen fabrics, for which colonial wool is now employed, and its relative value has sunk greatly.

To make amends for this, however, an increasing meat-eating population at home has considerably enhanced the value of the carcase, and a ready disposition to fatten, and attain early maturity, is a more important consideration now-a-days than the production of wool.

At one time, next to the wool obtained from Spain, the British short-woolled sheep supplied the best quality in Europe; the chief breeds from which it was obtained being the Wiltshire, Southdown, Ryeland, Dean-Forest, Mendip, Shropshire-Morf, and Shetland fleeces; some of these breeds having been crossed by the Spanish merino sheep, in the hope that it would turn out advantageously. But these expectations were not realised, the carcase of the merino sheep proving unprofitable, while they turned out bad nurses, and had fewer lambs than the old breeds of English sheep, but even then the influence of the growth of the German wool trades began to be felt, and according to the evidence brought before the Lords' Committee of Inquiry upon the subject in 1828, it went to prove that the wool of Saxony and Bohemia had entirely superseded the English short wool in our manufacture of fine cloth. The grower was however recompensed by an increased quantity of coarser wool under the new tactics pursued; and a larger carcase obtained, which could be sold profitably.

Although the introduction of the Spanish merino sheep into England must be looked upon as a failure upon the whole, it was not so in Germany, the Elector Augustus Frederick in 1765 having procured 300 rams and ewes from Spain, and in 1778 imported 400 more of the best breeds he could get from the same country.

His example was also followed by other European sovereigns, and amongst others George III., who has been styled the "farmer king," application having been made to the Crown of Spain, and at the beginning of the present century, and conclusion of the last, large numbers of the most celebrated Spanish breeds' were brought to England, which were distributed over various parts of the country, and put into the hands of the most enlightened agriculturists.

The attempt, although it succeeded in Germany, failed in England, owing to the superior value obtainable for a good carcase, which made this point of prominent importance; while on the Continent, its value did not rank so highly, the wool being the chief consideration; and with the advent of colonial wool in the market, the day was over for English wool to take the highest rank, and the improvement of the fleeces had to be abandoned in favour of that of the carcase.

The narration of these attempts at improvement through crossing the native breed of sheep with Spanish merinos have caused many facts to be recorded, which, though plainly evident in themselves, are often overlooked; such as the account given by Dr. Parry, of Bath, of the progressive amelioration of wool by the Spanish cross, but which relates to every quality alike, who says: " The first cross or a new breed gives to the lamb half of the ram's blood, or 50 per cent.; the second 75 per cent.; the third 87 per cent., and the fourth 93¾ per cent.; at which period it is said, that if the ewes have been judiciously selected, the difference of wool between the original stock and the mixed breed is scarcely to be discerned by the most able practitioners."

. Fink also points to similar conclusions in his *Treatise on the Rearing of Sheep in Germany, and the Improvement of Coarse Wool,* the following rules being promulgated:—

" To select at the commencement of the undertaking, the finest woolled rams and ewes that can be obtained for the first generation; for if those for the second race be finer than those used for the first, time will have been lost in effecting the proposed improvement.

" In like manner, to employ rams for the subsequent breeds quite equal to those for the first, or otherwise the intended improvement will be retarded.

"If an unimproved ewe be tupped by a ram of a mixed breed, and which has only one-fourth pure blood in him, the offspring will only have one-eighth of that race; and, by continuing to propagate in that manner, a complete separation of the two breeds will be at length effected."

29. PRELIMINARY MANAGEMENT OF SHEEP.—The preliminary step in stocking a farm with sheep is to obtain a breed which will thrive well upon the pasturage and soil whereon they are to be placed; the best results being obtained by producing sheep really good of their kind whatever that may be.

By careful selection in breeding, the sheep-farmer can develop the qualities he wishes to see in his flock, by choosing those animals conspicuous for robustness of constitution, rapid and large growth of fleece and carcase, symmetry of form, fecundity, and aptitude to fatten.

In every flock there will be found individual specimens which possess these desirable traits above the others; and in these the skilful breeder must find his materials for the gradual improvement of his entire stock; but unfortunately from the slovenly practice that very often prevails, matters are frequently left to chance which should have been directed by skilful observation and with a definite purpose in view.

When an alteration in the characteristics of a flock of sheep is sought to be brought about in making a change of blood, it is very necessary to make a right selection, and a few preparatory trials ought not to be begrudged upon an affair of such importance.

As a general rule, the most vigorous offspring is obtained by using shearling rams, and not allowing them to serve more than thirty ewes, the age and condition of the latter having much to do with the number of lambs dropped, and their vigorous condition.

Ewes generally produce their first lambs at two years old—though, as stated before, sometimes earlier—it not being thought expedient to allow them to breed before this time, nor after their fifth year, the frame of a yearling ewe being too immature to allow of her being a good mother, and of bringing up her progeny properly without permanent injury to her constitution. But even the stamina of ewes is much influenced by their method of living, and those of the hardier races that have been exclusively fed upon grass and hay, retain their teeth, and continue vigorous for two or three years longer than the heavier breeds that have been fostered upon a more artificial system of living, and have been partly fed upon turnips; and these may, in the ordinary current of affairs, be kept longer than the others for breeding purposes.

SHEARLING OXFORD DOWN.

30. DESCRIPTIVE NAMES OF SHEEP AT DIFFERENT AGES.—Sheep bear different names at different periods of their lives, which it may be as well to mention here. From the time of weaning to the first shearing, the males are called hogs, hoggets, or hoggerels; after which they are termed shearing, shearling, shearhog, or diamond-tups, or rams. After this they are termed two, three, or four-shear, according to the number of times they have undergone the shearing operation.

The castrated males, from the time of weaning to that of shearing, are termed wether, or wedder-hogs, then shearlings or shearings;

and after they have been shorn a second time, they are either called
young wethers, or two-shear wethers; then three, four, or five-shear
wethers, according to the number of shearings they have had.

The females are described as follows, at the different stages of
their existence. From the time of weaning to the first shearing,
they are termed ewe, or gimmer hogs; after then they take the
name of gimmers or theaves, which designation is applicable to
them only one year; after which time they are styled two, three, or
four-shear ewes, and when they become aged are termed *crones.*

31. FOR ASCERTAINING THE AGE OF SHEEP.—In buying
sheep when there may be some doubt as to their ages, it should be
remarked that sheep generally renew their first two teeth when
they are from fourteen to sixteen months old, and afterwards every
year about the same time until they have passed their third year,
or have become what is technically known as three-shear, and full-
mouthed. Still there is some doubt upon this point, for though
they have eight teeth in the under jaw, it has been surmised by
some that they only cast, or renew six inside ones, while others
maintain that the whole eight fore-teeth are renewed.

The successful breeding of sheep must a good deal depend upon
the quality of the pasture intended for their reception, and in old
times this was considered the principal feature in connection
with sheep-farming. The larger breeds are best calculated, as a
matter of course, for the richest and most luxurious grass, which is
to be found in the lowland grazing grounds; the smaller breeds
being adapted for the less fertile or mountainous districts, where
only the natural food for sheep, in the shape of grass, was to be
depended upon. But through skilful modern routine, the ordinary
condition of affairs can be very much modified in practice through
means of giving artificial food, which indeed can be carried to much
greater lengths than is commonly done, though adopted, and taken
full advantage of by some enlightened farmers.

Of late years a great outcry has been raised as to the unremu-
nerative character of farming, but it becomes a very pertinent
question whether farmers fully understand all the best methods of
taking advantage of the opportunities of keeping an increased
amount of live-stock upon their farms.

32. CLAY-LAND FARMERS AND TURNIP HUSBANDRY.—
Of late years it has been shown that clay-land farmers often labour
under a great disadvantage, because they cannot, as it is generally
supposed, avail themselves of the enormous advantages to be

derived from keeping a number of sheep on the land, because it will not grow turnips; and they cannot possess themselves of those improvements which result from the system known as the method of "turnip-husbandry."

But if stiff clay-land will not grow turnips, it will produce in abundance mangolds, cabbages, tares, and clover, and those crops eaten by sheep in yards, can be made to give a most satisfactory return both in mutton and manure.

The sheep by this method should go into yards about October, having sheds, the floors of which may be covered with burnt soil, which a few cwts. of coal will do as often as necessary when wanted to be renewed. A large amount of valuable manure will thus be accumulated, especially adapted for a cold clay-land, by the time spring comes round; and when straw is used, enough should be thrown down each day only in sufficient quantities to keep them clean, and the sheep will compress it by treading upon it, and fermentation thus be prevented; while if their feet be pared every six weeks they will not become lame.

ROMNEY MARSH RAM.

CHAPTER IV.

GENERAL MANAGEMENT.

General Management—Feeding—Summer Feeding—Folding—Winter Feeding—Turning Sheep into Pastures and Water Meadows—Pasturing Horses with Sheep—Liability to Rot—Uplands—Lowlands—Sheepcotes—Stells—Movable Folds—The Shepherd—The Shepherd's Dog—Statistics Relating to Sheep in the United Kingdom.

33. GENERAL MANAGEMENT.—The main thing in the profitable management of sheep is to keep them in such a manner as their rapid, uninterrupted progress may be ensured. Time is lost and food wasted when, from some cause or another, the progress of a flock is arrested; and this may be brought about, and often is, by unsuitable food and needless disturbance, as well as by the effects of unpropitious weather, as continued rainfall or severe snowstorms. Unremitting care and attention is always required for changing the green crops of a farm into so much good mutton and wool, but when this is well done, sheep-farming is a very profitable and an agreeable branch of husbandry.

In very inclement seasons, and especially upon clay soils, there is a great advantage to be obtained by feeding them in sheds that are well ventilated, but it has been observed that they make greater progress, in proportion, during the first six or eight weeks of their being brought under cover, than when they are thus kept for longer periods; and this circumstance indicates that this course is best to resort to in the case of sheep that are nearly ready for the market.

Cleanliness is very essential, if sheep are expected to thrive, and upon the system of *cotting*, the floors of the sheds should be covered with chalk well beaten in, if it is handy and easily procurable—laid upon a slight declivity, so that the urine may run off, and be saved by proper contrivances, made for the purpose, or burnt clay as before suggested.

34. FEEDING.— The system of feeding sheep upon turnips which now so largely prevails, is followed after several methods; one plan being to divide the land by hurdles, which will enclose as many sheep as they can clear in one day, advancing progressively until the whole field is cleared off.

Sometimes sheep are promiscuously turned into a turnip-field, and allowed to help themselves at will; but this plan will be seen to be wasteful, as a good many of the bulbs must inevitably be trodden underfoot, and spoiled a good deal by the excrement that is dropped.

Another method, which is generally considered the best, is to pull up as many turnips as the sheep can consume in one day, when they are admitted into the different enclosures; by which means the land becomes manured without the expense of having the manure carted thither.

Bakewell was averse to the system of folding sheep, considering that one part of a farm was enriched by this method, at the expense of the other. But it need not be pointed out that other kinds of manure can be resorted to for the portions upon which the sheep are not placed. His idea was, that where a large number of sheep are kept together, the strongest will always consume the best food, which ought to be appropriated by the least hardy.

35. SUMMER FEEDING.—On fallow land, in the spring months, after corn crops before turnips, sheep are sometimes folded; and when fed in summer upon artificial grasses, it has been found a good plan to take the sheep off their feed to lodge for the night elsewhere, to prevent the waste and injury to the food that would otherwise take place when they are left entirely upon it, and better still, to drive them off immediately after feeding, and so prevent them from lying down and spoiling a good deal of it.

As the digestive organs of the sheep are adapted for the consumption of comparatively dry and innutritious herbage, artificial grasses may be largely and profitably supplemented by the use of chaffed straw, which is often too much overlooked by farmers, whose profits might be largely increased by a more careful study of many economical contrivances that could be adopted in feeding stock.

Dry food is of the greatest possible service to sheep, both in winter and summer, and is frequently the means of preventing attacks of looseness of the bowels, occasioning the food to remain a longer time in the stomach, by which a larger amount of nourishment is obtained, and the risk of "hoving" is prevented, which is likely to be of common occurrence when the food is very succulent.

Intelligent farmers have found that, by using a large quantity of chaff for sheep, and folding all the roots on the land, that one-and-a-half sheep per acre can be kept against one sheep when chaff was not resorted to.

Of course little need be said when there is abundance of good natural pasture for the feed of sheep during the summer-time, but it is when the inclement season of winter sets in, and there are no natural grasses, that the art of the feeder is most called into account.

36. FOLDING.—The advantages and disadvantages of folding have often been canvassed, the practice being contended by some to be prejudicial to the animal at certain times, although advantageous to the land; while it is shown by others they could not profitably carry on the cultivation of their arable land without folding; the fact being that the circumstances of individual flock-masters vary very much.

In the *Survey of Somersetshire* the question is fairly put in the words of Mr. Billingsby, as follows : " In a rich fertile county where the quantity of arable land is small, and in mere subserviency to the grazing system, where dung is plenty, and can be put in the corn-land at a small expense, and where each sheep is highly fed, it is not to be wondered that the folding system should be held in derision and contempt; but I will be bold enough to repeat, that in a poor, exposed, and extensive corn-farm, the soil of which is light and stony, it is the *sine quâ non* of good husbandry. Let me ask its opponents whether the downs of Wilts and Dorset would wave with luxuriant corn if folding were abolished ? No. The farmer would plough and sow to little purpose were his fallows to remain untrod with the feet, and unmanured by the dung and perspiration of these useful animals. Besides, in the hot summer months nothing is so grateful to the flock itself as fresh ploughed ground; and sheep will, of their own accord, retire to it when their hunger is satisfied."

In Norfolk the oily matter contained in the fleece of sheep, which is communicated by their bodies to the land, and which is styled the "teathe," is much valued; and the general custom which now prevails in this respect, pretty well speaks as to the advantages realised by folding, more sheep being now supported upon arable than upon grass land.

When the land is wet, and turnips must necessarily be carted off, or on small farms where the flocks are too small to employ the services of a shepherd, it is a good plan to establish a standing fold in some dry, convenient spot, which would be found handiest when immediately adjoining the farm-buildings, which would thus afford a considerable amount of shelter in inclement seasons, and a large quantity of valuable food would be made, that could be transported to any part of the farm where it was most needed.

SHEARLING SHROPSHIRE.

37. WINTER FEEDING.—When sheep are fed upon turnips, it will be found desirable to use straw chaff, or some other dry food, as pea-haulm, of which they are uncommonly fond, to prevent looseness, or hoving. This latter sometimes occurs when the tops are very succulent, by which sheep are occasionally lost, and the straw-chaff counteracts the watery nature of the turnips. Straw-chaff also enables mangold-wurzel to be used at all seasons of the year, it not being considered desirable to use mangold alone during the winter months.

It has been found of great advantage to sheep to supplement

the bulk of their ordinary green food, or roots, with a small portion of bran, linseed-cake, or grain, which is found to promote the health of the flock, and to gradually bring them into a condition that will facilitate and further the fattening process.

Protection from the extremes of either heat or cold is also very desirable in the management of sheep. Trees certainly form an agreeable shade in summer, while they break the force of, and temper the winds in winter; but if the sheep seek shelter from the hot sun beneath them in summer-time, so do the flies also, from whose attacks the sheep suffer dreadfully at times; and a close thorn hedge, or a stone wall, in stony districts, affords as much protection as is necessary for a breeding flock. Where neither of these are to be had, recourse can always be made to hurdles thatched with straw; and an open fold, affording a rough shelter, can always be extemporised by erecting a double row of hurdles, and stuffing straw in between the interstices. Hurdles cleverly handled in this way may be made very subservient to the comfort of sheep during winter-time, as they can be lifted, and moved away when not wanted—a protection against cold winds and drifting rain being chiefly needed, which these are well capable of affording; the thick, woolly covering with which nature endows the sheep being a tolerably efficient protection against merely a cold atmosphere.

38. **TURNING SHEEP INTO PASTURES AND WATER MEADOWS.**—The month of May is considered the best time for turning sheep into summer pastures; the number of animals to be placed therein to be regulated according to the richness or poorness of the grass, for if too many are put upon pastures of insufficient quality to support the animals in a thriving and progressive condition, and they go back, it is difficult to pull them up again; and it is advisable rather to understock, on this account, than overstock.

At the same time, it must not be overlooked that the system of close-feeding is an advantageous one, for the plants being prevented from running up to seed, are preserved longer in the leaf; and will thus give a greater supply of food; while the coarse and unprofitable grasses are kept cropped down, and become more sweet and useful, chiming in with the rest of the feed.

The fine grasses that are produced on down-land are the best that can be furnished to sheep; but as these are not always to be had, and low-lying meadows have to be dealt with, sheep should be kept away from all grass that is subject to inundations, or otherwise they may become subject to rot.

39. **PASTURING HORSES WITH SHEEP.**— In damp situations, where coarse herbage springs up readily, it has been found a bad practice to pasture horses in the same field with sheep, on account of the tufts of long rank grass that spring up after the droppings of horses; unless the grass is allowed to be exposed first to a few nights' frost, after which the sheep may be admitted into the field. It is also, for the same reason, not advisable to allow sheep to eat the shoots which spring up from the shed grain amongst the stubble after harvest. They frequently, in fallow-land, draw up the plants by the roots, which they eat with the dirt adhering to them; and when there is an insufficient supply of food of a proper description, they consume the lesser spearwort and the marsh pennywort, which spring up in moist situations.

40. **LIABILITY TO ROT.**—When sheep are turned into water meadows, or any other place where there may be a danger of their being subject to rot, they should be first fed with some dry food, as straw-chaff, or hay; and then, when the heavy dews have been evaporated by the rays of the sun, gently drive them round the field for some time before suffering them to feed.

When dry food is given, pure water also should be supplied, especially in the height of summer, when the heat is intense, and the grass very dry and destitute of succulence.

We could considerably enlarge upon this subject, but our space will not allow us to give more than the general outlines of the salient points to be observed in feeding sheep—a practice which admits of so many variations, each of which must in a measure depend upon the class of land at the disposal of the sheep-farmer; but in stocking a farm with sheep, care should be taken to know precisely what its exact capabilities are, the pasturage and soils being so highly diversified in various parts of the country.

41. **UPLANDS.**—Naturally the short-woolled races of sheep are best adapted for upland and hilly pastures, but it has been found extremely desirable to couple short-woolled ewes with Leicester, or long-woolled rams; by which a double advantage is secured. The sheep raised from these crosses, when equally well fed, attain to nearly the size of the pure lowland breeds; while the ewes being more hardy and prolific, and also better nurses than lowland ewes, a union of good points is thus effected; and the hill sheep-farmer is enabled to bring to market a higher class of animal than he

otherwise would have been enabled to do, and such sheep when sold to be placed upon pastures of a lower altitude invariably do well. Southdown ewes, crossed by a long-woolled ram, form a very favourite blending of characteristics with most English flockmasters. In the mountainous districts of the north of England and Scotland, Cheviot ewes, or Black-faced ewes of the Heath breed, crossed by a Leicester ram, are generally found very suitable in those situations where an improved breed may safely be reared, and there is some-thing else to depend upon than merely scanty and coarse herbage, fit only for Heath sheep.

42. **LOWLANDS.**— In the lower and good pastures of some counties, the Romney Marsh, the Bamptons, and other long-woolled breeds will be found to answer well, as the amount of natural feed to be found in such situations is more abundant; and this can be supplemented to an almost unlimited extent by the artificial grasses, pulped roots and straw-chaff, cabbages, &c. A Bampton crossed by a Leicester is a good breed for rich lands on a low level, being found suitable and profitable, the animals being ready for the butcher at twenty months old, and weighing 20 lbs., or more, per quarter.

43. **SHEEPCOTES.**—Sheepcotes, to afford warmth and pro-tection to sheep, may be easily and cheaply constructed by those who like them (many considering them objectionable), by planting rough posts in the ground, and filling up the spaces with furze, and putting on a rough roof, and thatching it with the same material, or straw; and rough racks to hold the fodder may be easily con-structed, and the whole managed for a comparatively trifling outlay. The floor should be laid with gravel, burnt clay, or rubble, rammed down hard, so as to cause it to always remain dry.

At lambing time these cotes are unquestionably of service; but, as before remarked in another place, they sometimes cause sheep to be attracted to them, and cause them to remain under cover, instead of being abroad, seeking their living.

44. **STELLS.**—In mountainous and bleak districts, flockmasters erect open folds, which are termed " stells," as a protection against the inclemency of the weather. The shape of the stells is a very material point—being either of the form of the letter T, H, or S ; the object being to guard against the wind, from whatever quarter it might blow, the circular shape being found very useful in situations where the snow is apt to drift. The wind whirls con-stantly round it during a violent storm, and so prevents the snow

from lodging within the fence; the snow-drifts in some exposed districts overpowering the animals, which are often buried beneath them.

45. **MOVABLE FOLDS.**—The advantage in using movable folds consists in the fact, that land can be regularly manured without any expense beyond shifting the hurdles. Being, however, mostly pitched upon arable land, the dirt and wet are sometimes

SHEEP FOLDING HURDLE.

This Illustration, and that on page 69, are kindly lent us by Messrs. Bayliss, Jones, and Bayliss, of Wolverhampton.

injurious to the wool of the sheep; and if placed at too great a distance from the pastures, sometimes the labour of travelling backwards and forwards prevents the sheep from fattening.

The standing-fold is an excellent plan where the land is wet, as before described, though the land is deprived of the supposed advantages resulting from the teathe, and there is the expense of removing the manure, while the stells are only applicable and necessary in those districts exposed to the ravages of mountain snow-storms.

46. **THE SHEPHERD.**—The shepherd should be an experienced man, competent to administer any of the surgical remedies for the

mitigation of diseases that are usually attendant upon a flock; and the best shepherds are those who have commenced their duties early in life, who, from long experience and observation, have acquired the necessary knowledge demanded in the care of sheep, and are at the same time active, careful, and good-tempered in herding them, and in working amongst their charges. A good-tempered man, aided by a close-mouthed dog, will do his work in half the time that it takes a passionate man to effect it; the property under his care demanding constant and unswerving attention.

A good man solely employed in shepherding, it has been considered, can manage and keep in good order during the summer months, and under common grazing in grass pastures or clover, a flock of 800 sheep.

In the winter, however, he could only manage 500 with difficulty, 400 being enough if they were fed upon turnip-keeping, a good deal of labour being incurred in moving the hurdles, and dragging up the turnip-hulls from the ground.

47. **THE SHEPHERD'S DOG.**—The intelligent animals that are trained to assist the shepherd, perform a very important part in the care of the flock, and spare the shepherd's legs, in keeping the sheep together, and preventing them from straying. There are ordinarily two recognised species of animals employed as sheep-dogs, though cross-bred dogs are common enough—the kind usually met with in England, and the shag-haired "collie." These are, however, excelled by the Spanish sheep-dogs, which never bite the sheep, as English and Scotch dogs do, but are so gentle with them that, when danger threatens, instead of shunning them, the sheep will gather round them for protection.

In Spain, and on many parts of the Continent, it is noticeable how little *driving* is necessary—the sheep *following* the shepherd, and not being driven with the violence that unfortunately may often be seen displayed in this country, and the barking and yelling resorted to by man and dog conjointly.

48. **STATISTICS RELATING TO SHEEP IN THE UNITED KINGDOM.**—The agricultural returns which are issued every year by the English Government, furnish a statistical account of the number of sheep in Great Britain, and the relative position of this important branch of agricultural enterprise.

The number of sheep recorded by these returns for the year 1879, shows a small increase over 1878, but not enough to counterbalance the falling-off in lambs, amounting to 366,000 in Great Britain.

E

With few exceptions, the report of the lambing season of 1878 was very unfavourable; and in Scotland, the severity of the weather during the winter and spring, caused a diminution of sheep as well.

The number of sheep and lambs in Great Britain during the year 1879, is set down as being much the same as in that of 1877—namely, 28,157,000, as against 28,161,000; and the numbers have been less only in two years since 1867—namely, in 1871 and 1872. In Ireland, the returns of cattle show a small increase, and of sheep a small decrease; cattle numbering 4,067,000, and sheep 4,017,000, which strikingly illustrates the relatively greater number of cattle over sheep that are kept in Ireland.

Accounts have also been furnished from Australia, including New Zealand, of the numbers of live stock; by which it appears that there are more than a million horses in Australia, which is a very large number in comparison with the population. The number of horned cattle was more than seven millions and a quarter, and of sheep about 61,000,000. The numbers of both cattle and sheep were much diminished through the drought of 1877-78; but in most of the colonies, at the time this report was issued, the losses had been repaired, though in Victoria and in Queensland the number of sheep showed a still further falling-off, owing, it is stated as regards the latter, to the drought of the past season. The decrease in the sheep in Queensland has, however, been continuous since 1868, up to the time the report above spoken of refers to, numbering nearly nine millions in 1868, compared with five-and-a-half millions in 1879.

FAT TAILED SHEEP.

HEATH RAM.

CHAPTER V.

BREEDING, ETC.

Breeding—Time of Coupling—Number of Ewes to a Ram—Period of Gestation—
Yeaning—Management of Lambs—Weaning—Selection of Lambs—Marking
—Washing—Shearing—Dipping Lambs.

49. BREEDING.—Where breeding is aimed at and made a
leading feature, there are, in every flock, individual specimens of
animals which possess finer points and qualities than others; these
being robustness of constitution; rapid and large growth of fleece;
aptitude to fatten; and fecundity. These should be carefully selected, and by using them only for breeding, the standard of quality
of a flock must be inevitably raised; and where this has been
established, to avoid breeding too much "in-and-in," which is
unfavourable to the health and vigour of a flock, fresh blood should
be introduced, so as not to breed continuously from animals of too
near consanguinity, though this must necessarily be done in the first
instance. Before coupling the sheep, each should be examined in
the minutest manner, and those animals in which there is any short-
coming, or defect, should be unhesitatingly rejected. This applies
equally to both ram and ewe, but especially the male; and where
points may be deficient in the female, choice should be made of a
ram which is unusually good in those where the ewe is deficient.

A good ram may always be procured with comparative ease, but
no ewes should be made use of that are tainted with any hereditary
disease, which often appears in the form of gumminess of wool,

which attracts the fly; boils about the face and neck; or yellowness of the skin.

Even what are regarded very often as casual circumstances, that are objectionable, should be taken into account, for it has been observed that sheep struck with the fly one year, are invariably so the next, and will often continue to be thus affected for successive years; and by choosing both ewes and rams judiciously in this way, the flockmaster will find himself amply repaid for the trouble he has taken.

50. **TIME OF COUPLING.**—The time at which the ram is admitted to the ewe depends to a certain extent upon the nature of the climate, and the prospect of spring food, ewes being generally fit to breed at about fifteen to eighteen months; much too depends upon the forward state of the flock, or otherwise, the usual time being about the commencement of October; in East Sussex, during the last fortnight in October or the first week in November; and in West Sussex, at the beginning of September. In the county of Dorset, where the ewes bring lambs twice in the year, and in some of the south and south-western districts, where house-lamb is raised, the system is varied, and the ram is admitted so that the lambs are dropped a month or six weeks earlier; in exposed situations the beginning of November is considered early enough. The majority of British sheep, excepting the Dorsets aforesaid, cannot be induced to take the ram before September.

51. **NUMBER OF EWES TO A RAM.**—The number of ewes to be put to a ram depends in some degree upon the nature of the farm, as well as being regulated by the ram's age and vigour. In mountainous districts three rams are put to a hundred ewes; while in the lowlands, in enclosed pastures, two are considered quite sufficient—sixty ewes being generally considered about the proper average; fifty or sixty being quite enough when the rams are young, but as they grow older the number of ewes may be increased. When a young ram is put to too great a number of ewes, the lambs are not only likely to be deficient in number, but inferior in strength to those where proper precautions have been taken.

No ram should be used that is not sound and vigorous, nor till after he has become a shearling; and he will continue in his prime till he is five years old, but should not be used after he has attained his sixth year, and before being thus used, in the first instance, he should be previously well fed, so as to be got in high condition.

52. PERIOD OF GESTATION.—The period of gestation is roundly estimated to last twenty-one weeks. M. Tessier, who made an exhaustive series of experiments upon the period of gestation of most domestic animals, has recorded the result of upwards of nine hundred ewes, of which the date they were served by the ram was severally noted :—

> 140 lambed between the 146th and 150th day;
> 676   ,,   ,,   150th and 154th ,,
> 90   ,,   ,,   154th and 161st ,,

Which gives an extreme of fifteen days, the average showing a duration of about 152 days, as nearly as possible, or nearly twenty-two weeks.

53. YEANING.—The usual time of yeaning is about the end of March or beginning of April, and during the period of gestation they should receive a considerable amount of attention, and, if possible, be placed in tolerably good, sheltered pastures, where they are not likely to be exposed to be frightened or hurt ; and as the time of yeaning approaches, the care and attention of the shepherd should be redoubled, lest any accident should befall them which would cause them to slip their lambs.

The ewes when put to the ram should be in fair, but not high, condition, and during the time of gestation they should not be allowed to get absolutely fat, as there would be a difficulty in lambing ; while, on the other hand, they should not be too poor, as it is essential they should have the necessary strength to go through it, as well as having an adequate supply of milk for the support of their lambs.

When sheep are kept upon downs and upon mountainous grazings, the ewes are commonly left to lamb in the open field without any protection ; the watchful care of the shepherd being exercised to render assistance when necessary. Some flockmasters take the precaution of providing enclosures which are mounted on wheels, and can be drawn wherever they are needed. Others put up some movable covered pens—which may easily be constructed out of hurdles—which are littered with straw or fern, and made perfectly dry, open to the ewes so that they can range the pastures and return to the pens whenever they are disposed ; but wherever the sheep are placed, choice should always be made of a level piece of pasture free from all ruts, holes, or ditches, which often cause difficulties.

As a rule, it is safe practice not to allow too plentiful a supply of food to the ewes for three or four weeks previous to lambing, as if in too thriving a state, gangrene sometimes follows after parturition, on account of the blood being in au inflamed conditiou.

This high feeding is sometimes practised with a view of ensuring a plentiful supply of milk, which although, as stated before, is necessary in a certain measure or degree, may with greater safety be urged on five or six days after the event.

As a rule, Nature does not require to be assisted, but sometimes labour will be difficult, when the services of an experienced shep-

EWE PEN.

herd will need to be called into requisitiou; and when yeaning has been long in its duration, and the ewe has become exhausted, warm gruel should be given to it, and it should be kept separate in quiet quarters away from the rest of the flock, until it has recovered.

54. **MANAGEMENT OF LAMBS.**—Sometimes the lambs when dropped will appear to be in an almost lifeless condition, and a good deal of attention is necessary to restore them to animation, and a hut with a chimney in it, with a fire, and convenience for warming milk, is found to be very handy at yeaning-time for the shepherd to make use of; lambs that to all appearance were dead having been brought round by being laid for a few hours in a warm

basket, placed near a fire; and a little warm milk poured occasionally down their throats.

Although it is very rarely the case, the ewe sometimes deserts her lamb, or dies in giving birth to it; when it becomes necessary to put it to a ewe that has lost her own, or bring it up by hand on cow's milk.

When the tup lambs have acquired sufficient strength, which will be generally when about eight or ten days old, those not intended to be kept as rams should be castrated. The weather should be dry and mild for this operation, and towards evening is considered the best time for it to be done.

When it is customary to cut the tails of lambs, they should be docked about this time, but some flockmasters whose sheep are placed in exposed situations refrain from docking the ewes, considering that a long, bushy tail affords a considerable protection to the udder, though some again contend that this is counterbalanced by the long tail being found in the way at yeaning-time.

The lambs are allowed to run in the pastures with the ewes, weather permitting; for which purpose the best are selected, if it is the intention of getting rid of the ewes, and selling them to the butcher, and are fed upon turnips and rape, with hay and bruised oil-cake, if the pastures are not sufficiently rich.

55. **WEANING.**—If lambs are dropped early in the season and the weather remains cold, they are allowed to remain a longer time with the ewe, but lambs are usually weaned in the early part of July, and should not be postponed till later than the end of the month, unless they were dropped late in the spring. Nothing more is required to be done than separating the lambs from the ewes, driving them so far apart that their different bleatings may not be heard by each other.

56. **SELECTION OF LAMBS.**—Particular care should be exercised in the selection of the ewe lambs, and any that are at all ill-formed, or possess any defect, should on no account be kept, but got rid of; even the weaker lambs should be separated from the stronger, and dealt with in a suitable manner, and any that appear constitutionally defective should be sent to the butcher.

After they have been separated from the ewes, each lamb should be carefully examined, in order to see whether it may have received any injury, and be put aside for curative treatment.

57. **MARKING.**—Lambs are marked in various ways, according to the fancy of their owners, as well as sheep, by a brand upon the

cheek, or notches in the ears, or with ruddle or tar upon the fleece, distinguishing the two sexes by marking them respectively on the *near* or *off* sides; and, when removed, are put upon the best pastures, or the aftermath of crops of clover, lucerne, or sainfoin, spring tares, or any crop of a similar nature that is nourishing and calculated to stimulate their growth, the aim being always for improvement to be progressive; and they should be shifted whenever a fresh bite becomes necessary. Upon the approach of winter, when the herbage begins to fail, they should then be put upon turnips, rape, and other food best adapted to the object in view; but great care should be taken not to suffer them to touch either turnips or clover when the frost is upon them.

58. **WASHING.**—Preparatory to being shorn, sheep are washed, with the object of removing from the fleece the dirt and grit with which the wool is encumbered, which heightens its value, and puts it into better condition for manufacturing purposes. For the convenience of washing, it is generally usual to form wash-dikes in small streams, or rivulets, two or three feet in depth, pointing against the current, in order that the water, as it is soiled in the washing, may flow away from the sheep. Or a dam is placed against the current in a convenient place, with a flood-gate in the middle, by which the water is retained or let off at pleasure; on the one side a pen is formed for the washing, and on the other a path is hurdled in for the sheep to pass away when the washing is done.

The pen, or artificial pool, is railed round with one rail the height of the water, beneath which the sheep is thrust under with a long pole called a *poy*, with which the operator either pulls the sheep to him, or pushes it away, as required.

59. **SHEARING.** — Sheep are usually shorn, in a fine season, in the early part of June, and though the operation is sometimes deferred until later with the idea of gaining a heavier fleece, yet it is not wise to defer it, as the earlier it is done the better, as the growth of the wool prevents the attack of flies, which are often very troublesome and destructive, especially in enclosed and woody counties, at an advanced season. The proper period for clipping, or shearing, must a good deal depend upon the season, the effects of the advance of which should be watched, which will be indicated as soon as the young wool has sufficiently raised the old fleece from the skin, when it should be shorn.

The old-fashioned method of shearing was to do it longitudinally; but this method was both attended with some little difficulty, and was seldom neatly executed, there generally being an ounce or two of wool left on each sheep, which was calculated to impair the growth of the next year's wool. By clipping the wool circularly—shearing round the body of the sheep—the work is more uniformly executed.

When using the shears great care is necessary, so as not to wound or prick the animal with the edge or point of the shears, as the flies will attack the wounded part. The effects of such accidents are guarded against by smearing the cut with turpentine or some healing salve, as tallow and tar.

After shearing, the flock should be carefully looked over repeatedly, in order to examine if the flies have deposited any of their larvæ; and if it is found they have deposited any of their eggs, the tumours should be opened, and mercurial ointment rubbed in, which will destroy the insect.

The following unguent has been very commonly used in order to kill the lice and ticks, which is rubbed over every part of the body with a currying-brush :—

> Train oil .... 4 gallons.
> Oil of tar .... ½ ,,
> Oil of turpentine .... 1 pint.

60. DIPPING LAMBS.—As it is very desirable to get rid of the annoyance of ticks and lice from the flock—and when the sheep have been shorn there is no shelter for these vermin, so that if they can be cleared from the lambs, the flock will have got rid of the plague during the whole succeeding year — to effect this object the lambs are dipped in a solution made of the following ingredients :—One pound of arsenic is dissolved in boiling soapsuds, and then poured into a large tub with a considerable quantity of warm water.

In this mixture, which is about sufficient for twenty lambs, each is immersed singly, and then dried as well as possible, by squeezing the water out of the wool by the hand. One immersion will destroy the lice, and will keep them free during the following summer from fly and maggots, but precautions must be taken that their heads are not pushed under water during the operation, in case they should swallow some of the poisoned water.

SHEPHERD'S DOG.

CHAPTER VI.

THE DISEASES OF SHEEP.

Diseases of Sheep, and their Remedies—Flies –The Bot—The Fluke—The Rot—
The Tick—Foot-rot—The Epidemic—Consumption—Hoove, Blasting, or
Hoven—Obstructions in the Gullet—Distension of the Rumen—Concretions
in the Stomach—Diarrhœa—Diarrhœa in Lambs—Dysentery, or Braxy—
Catarrh—Bronchitis—Pleurisy—Pneumonia—Red-water—Small-pox — Black-
muzzle—The Scab—Turn-sick—Giddiness—Inflammation of the Brain—
Palsy—Apoplexy—Inflammation of the Bladder—Ailments of the Udder—
Sore Teats—Diseases peculiar to Ewes.

61. **DISEASES OF SHEEP, AND THEIR REMEDIES.**—We
have already made allusion to flies, maggots, and ticks in sheep;
and we shall commence a brief notice of the various diseases to
which they are subject, by referring to these pests.

62. **FLIES, &o.**—Flesh-flies lay their eggs upon the skin of the
sheep, where in time they hatch and produce maggots, and unless
they are properly attended to during the course of the spring and
summer, a fatal termination will result.

The fattest sheep are generally the first that are singled out for
attack by the flies, especially when the skin is broken or scratched;
but the mischief likely to ensue may be prevented by constantly
clipping, cleaning, and anointing the maggoty parts. There are
several species of the large flesh-flies, some being black, others
white and greenish; the root of the tail, and immediately round the
anus, or those parts where excrement may have been hanging,

being the most likely places to be infected, though the back is often visited as well.

These parts should be clipped about a month previously to shearing-time, as a safeguard against their visitation, and about a couple of months afterwards as well, and the rump and buttocks washed with the following liquid, which will in all probability prevent the breeding of maggots :—

One pound of arsenic finely powdered, 12 ozs. of potash, 6 ozs. common yellow soap, 30 gallons of soft water. These should be boiled together for a quarter of an hour, and care should be taken not to inhale the steam.

63. THE BOT (*Œstrus ovis*), is often a dreadful scourge amongst a flock, the large maggots, or hydatids residing in the frontal sinus for a considerable period, producing vertigo, staggers, and death, on account of finding their way to the brain.

Trepanning has been recommended, and a wire has been thrust up the nostril to destroy the bladder in which the bot is; but it is the best course to kill the animals when seized by the disease.

64. THE FLUKE (*Fasciola hepatica*) causes the rot, which consists of those parasites which are sometimes called *plaice*, from the resemblance they bear to the flat fish of that name, which are found floating about the biliary ducts, apparently feeding on the bile (varying in size from an eighth to a quarter-of-an-inch in diameter), which prevents the bile from performing its allotted functions in the animal economy; their minute eggs being deposited on the grass, from whence they are taken into the system.

65. THE ROT, which is the result of the presence of the parasites above referred to, does not at once show its unfavourable symptoms, for sheep have been known actually to improve for a short time, after which the evil effects of the visitation are made manifest. When the disease is established, it is usual to hurry on the fattening process, by giving the most nutritious food, as oil-cake and linseed, accompanied with salt given daily, which has a remedial effect, as is proved by sheep which are fed upon salt marshes, that are overflowed by spring-tides, doing well in rotting seasons; superabundant moisture either in food, soil, or situation, being supposed to be the real cause of this malady.

66. THE TICK (*Melophagus ovinus*).—This troublesome pest is best got rid of in the way suggested under the heading of "Dipping Lambs," the insect supporting its own life by sucking the sheep, and especially lambs; the females depositing their larvæ amongst

the wool. The somewhat singular, but by no means unusual, sight of a starling being perched upon a sheep's back, and busily engaged amongst the wool thereof, is due to the friendly office that is being performed of picking out the ticks.

67. **FOOT-ROT.**—The parts which connect the hoof with the bones of the foot is the seat of this disease, which mostly arises from the foot being exposed to too great an amount of moisture,

SPECKLED FACED MOUNTAIN SHEEP.

when the horn not being worn away by attrition, becomes soft, and is easily penetrated by gravel and stones; sometimes the upper part where it is thinnest being detached from its connections. Inflammation and ulceration often follow, and run under the foot, and the hoof is at times entirely lost, so that the foot—still being exposed to wet—forms fungous granulations, and in its worst state a shocking condition of disease is produced.

The feet should be protected from moisture, and the ragged parts of the foot pared away, and a caustic applied to promote healthy action in the diseased part.

After paring, the following mixture will be found to promote the healthy growth of the horn, while at the same time protecting the foot from moisture:—

Tar .... 8 ozs.
Lard........................ 4 „

melted together, and when these are incorporated thoroughly, add

Oil of turpentine ...... ½ oz.
Sulphuric acid .... ½ „

mixed carefully with the above.

68. THE EPIDEMIC.—Though arising from different causes, the Epidemic, as it is called, bears a very close resemblance to the foot-rot in sheep, but arises from fever in the system. The feet feel hard previous to the formation of matter, which is the result of inflammation, the symptoms being a great soreness between the claws, a separation between the hoof at its upper part and the parts beneath taking place.

The best course of treatment is to give cooling medicines, such as Epsom salts; and treat the feet in the same way as that prescribed for foot-rot.

69. CONSUMPTION.—Excess of moisture, or too much watery food, as turnips alone, often lay the seeds of consumption, although not immediately traced ; another reason why dry food, such as chaffed straw, should be given with roots.

It mostly appears in ewes after lambing, for although the yeaning may have been got over easily and without any difficulty, they have afterwards gradually pined and lost appetite, dying about a month after lambing. As may be seen, an insidious disease of this nature may affect the health and stamina of the succeeding flock. No cure can be suggested for a disease where the vital organs are already sapped before its presence is suspected, and preventive measures can only be used. Excessive wet, which may be guarded against in a measure, by occasional housing, or keeping the sheep in as dry a situation as possible, are the best courses to adopt. Not giving *too* many turnips, and avoiding giving them when the surfaces of the roots and the shaws are unduly wet.

To guard against the effects of wet, and keep the system vigorous and strong by supplying internal warmth, a little concentrated food will be found of great advantage and productive of animal heat.

70. HOOVE, BLASTING, OR HOVEN.—This is occasioned by sheep being put too suddenly upon green, succulent food; which causes the rumen to be distended with gas, caused by its fermentation. Or it may take place through accident, when sheep have obtained access to a field of broad clover ; the danger being greatest at night, or early in the morning, when the hoar frost is on the ground.

The sudden ehange from eommon turnips to.swedes will sometimes produce it, and a prompt remedy must be applied, and the hollow probang passed into the rumen in order to allow the gases to eseape through it.

If this is not to hand upon an emergency, a dessert-spoon of salt should be dissolved and poured down the throat, salt being almost always at hand; but a drachm, or more, of chloride of lime is better still. When there is no time to administer medicine of any kind, such as doses of two drachms of sulphuric ether, the trochar should be plunged into the rumen through the flank, or a penknife in the absence of the former; if the latter is used, a stick of elder with the pith pushed out, or a quill, should be kept in the wound so as to allow of the escape of gas.

Even after relief has been obtained by puncturing, it is advisable to give the medicine recommended, as an accumulation of gas often takes place again, and indigestion follows, as well as sub-acute hoven; and under these circumstances the following will be found a useful medicine:—

Ginger............................	2 drachms.
Chloride of lime	1 scruple.
Gentian	1 drachm.
Magnesia	2 ozs.

As the digestive organs will be thrown considerably out of order, great care should be used in feeding, and salt sprinkled over green food will be found of advantage.

71. **OBSTRUCTIONS IN THE GULLET.**—Sheep are oeeasionally subjeet to obstructions in the gullet, arising from a piece of turnip or other food, whieh pressing upon the wind-pipe, impedes the passage of air to and from the lungs ; though these oeeasions of distress are less frequent than with eows or oxen. The probang must be passed over the roof of the tongue into the gullet, having been first previously oiled, and pressed gently along, when the obstrueting particle ean be generally pushed on into the rumen.

To do this with the greatest amount of eonvenienee, the head of the sheep should be held between a man's knees, in the proper position, so that the probang does not lacerate the sides of the œsophagus. If this fails, there is nothing else but a dangerous operation—whieh must be performed by a veterinary surgeon—of eutting into the œsophagus, and taking away the obstruction.

72. **DISTENSION OF THE RUMEN.**—Distension of the rumen is of mueh rarer occurrence with sheep than with oxen, but when the digestive organs are inclined to be out of order, too hastily eating roots will sometimes produce it, and the abdomen, though not distended to so great an extent as in the ease of blasting, will be hard and firm,

According to circumstances, the probang and stomach-pump are sometimes respectively made use of, and bleeding is resorted to, after which liquids are administered with the object of softening the contents of the rumen, an accumulation being often impacted in it which has got hard.

73. **CONCRETIONS IN THE STOMACH.**—As sheep feed largely upon plants which more or less have earth attached to their roots, they must necessarily at times swallow a good deal, which does not, as a rule, have any injurious effect; but on the contrary, is thought most likely to have a useful effect in neutralising the acidity of the stomach, but sometimes when too much has been swallowed, inflammation of the intestines or coats of the stomachs is produced.

Saline purgatives are the best to administer, as sulphate of magnesia; as well as vegetable tonics. In the stomachs of lambs towards autumn, balls are sometimes found which are felted together, consisting of fibres of wool and the hard food commingled with mucus.

74. **DIARRHŒA.**—Diarrhœa, sometimes called *flux* or *scouring*, is mostly confined to hoggets and young sheep, and is often brought about by their being taken from somewhat poor pastures and put upon rich ones. It is not considered very injurious, but may prove so if it is long continued, or if it arises from wet, when they should be removed to a dry pasture and be supplied with good hay.

Young lambs, when only a fortnight or three weeks old, are attacked by it, under the name of *gall*, caused by eating the grass which springs up after fertilising showers.

A good diarrhœa mixture is made of the following:—

Catechu powdered.....................	4 drachms.
Prepared chalk powdered	1 oz.
Ginger powdered	2 drachms.
Opium powdered	½ ::

This, mixed in peppermint water (about half a pint), should be given twice a day, in doses of two or three tablespoonfuls for a sheep, and half that quantity for a lamb.

75. **DIARRHŒA IN LAMBS.**—There is, however, in lambs diarrhœa arising from different causes, the *white skit*, so called from the pale colour of the fæces, not really arising from looseness, but constipation, and is caused by the coagulation of the milk in the fourth stomach, where it will accumulate until it amounts to several pounds, the whey passing off by the bowels, which causes the appearance to which it owes its name.

Alkalies should be given to dissolve this hardened mass, the internal membrane of the stomach abounding in muriatic acid. Half an ounce of magnesia dissolved in water, or a quarter of an ounce of hartshorn mixed with water, should be repeatedly given, and Epsom salts afterwards. A rather large quantity of water should be used with the medicines.

The *green skit*, so named to mark its distinction from the *white skit*, is occasioned by the lambs being turned with their mothers, into rich pastures, and arises from the greater stimulus given to their digestive organs, and will often pass off; at times it being prudent to give two drachms of Epsom salts, followed by the cordial medicine first named under the heading of diarrhœa.

76. **DYSENTERY, OR BRAXY.**—This is much more dangerous than diarrhœa, arising from inflammation of the coats of the stomach, a sudden change of pasturage from a moist succulent one to a high and dry one sometimes producing it, or coming on after being exposed to wet and cold after travelling.

The dung is hard and smaller in quantity than usual, though frequently evacuated, smells offensively, and is covered with mucus and blood.

Linseed gruel should be administered several times a-day, and medicine composed of the following ingredients should be given :—

> Linseed oil.................................... 2 ozs.
> Powdered opium .... 2 grains.

given in linseed tea.

The following day the opium should be given alone, with a scruple of powdered ginger, and two scruples of gentian, and the oil again given if required.

77. **CATARRH.**—Sheep are very subject to catarrh towards autumn, particularly in wet seasons, or when the flock has been driven from one part to another, and has been exposed to changes of the weather very much.

Catarrh will sometimes last several weeks, and then get well of itself, shelter and good nursing helping this onwards; the improvement of the animal naturally being retarded while it lasts.

In mild cases, a little gruel will be found useful, combined with the shelter as mentioned; but if the symptoms are severe, half an ounce of Epsom salts, a drachm each of nitre and ginger, and half a drachm of tartarised antimony dissolved in gruel, should be given. Bleeding from the neck is practised in severe cases.

78. **BRONCHITIS.**—Sheep are not often troubled with bronchitis, but similar effects are sometimes due to the presence of worms in the windpipe. The treatment should consist in giving half a pint of lime-water to a sheep, and a gill to a lamb, every

morning and evening, and for a week; or give two teaspoonfuls of salt dissolved in water.

79. **PLEURISY.**—This disorder is characterised by symptoms of inflammation, pain, and fever, and mostly arises from a chill given to the systeı   the disorder sometimes exhibiting itself after sheep-washing. Leicester sheep are said to be more liable to pleurisy than any other breed.

80. **PNEUMONIA.**— Narrow-chested sheep, when kept upon water-meadows, are said to be most liable to this disease, as the Dorset breed—as well as the Leicesters, which are, on the contrary, *wide-chested;* but of this there is no positive proof, as the opposite characteristics of the two breeds would tend to show, although some breeds may be possibly more tender than others in the lungs, the disorder being in reality inflammation of the lungs.

Bleeding from the neck is generally prescribed, and purgatives given, succeeded by sedative medicine, which may be composed of the following :—

> Nitrate of potash........................ 1 drachm.
> Tartarised antimony .... 10 grains.
> Ipecacuanha.......................... 5   „

81. **REDWATER.**—Redwater in sheep is a different disorder to that of the same name in cattle, consisting, in the case of the former, of an effusion of red serum or water in the abdomen.

Young lambs are somewhat subject to it before weaning, as well as afterwards; and it often occurs after the ground has been covered with hoar frosts, and the sheep have been feeding upon turnips; and is supposed to arise either from cold, watery food, or lying upon the cold ground.

It is a dangerous disease, the symptoms being loss of appetite and rumination, dullness of habit, costiveness, and occasional giddiness; the progress of the disorder being so rapid that lambs apparently well over night have been found dead in the morning.

If an affected animal is in anything like condition, it will be the best plan to kill it; but if treatment is resorted to, the following will be found an appropriate medicine:—

> Opium powdered...................... ½ drachm.
> Ginger   „   .... 1 oz.
> Sulphate of magnesia .... 1 lb.
> Gentian powdered .... 1 oz.

This will be enough for ten sheep, dissolved in warm water, or given in gruel.

82. **SMALL-POX.**—Small-pox is fortunately a rare disease in this country, though it has been imported from abroad occasionally. The symptoms are dulness of the eyes, accompanied with swelling of the eyelids, succeeded by reddish spots on the naked places;

F

the animal having a dull and moping appearance. After a few days, swellings something like flea-bites appear, varying in size ; in severe cases being of a purple hue, and running into one another. Small-pox is presented under two aspects : the distinct and the confluent ; the latter being the worst phase.

It is dreadfully contagious, and little can be done in the way of medicine ; warmth and shelter, plenty of water, and febrifuge medicines, with gruel and tonics, being the best remedies ; but the most prudent course to pursue, upon the first breaking out of the disorder, would be to destroy those sheep at once that are infected, to prevent contagion, as only partial remedies can be adopted.

83. **BLACK MUZZLE.**—An eruption sometimes takes place upon the face and nose of sheep, which is known by the name of "black muzzle" in some districts, which is caused by the sour nature of some kinds of herbage.

An ointment composed of the following ingredients will be found to cure the eruption :—

Hog's lard...	1 lb.
Powdered alum	4 drachms.
Sulphate of zinc powdered	4 drachms.

and applied to the affected parts.

84. **THE SCAB.**—The scab is due to the presence of insects (*acari*), which burrow beneath the skin, and cause great irritation ; being of a similar nature to the mange in dogs and horses, produced, in the first place, by poverty and filth, and afterwards spread by contagion.

About twelve days after becoming infected, the sheep will commence to rub themselves against some hard object or other, removing the wool in the action, and getting out of condition from the self-imposed labour, and the uneasiness caused, and hard pimples will form, and the skin feel rough. These pustules get broken, and a scab forms, which leaves a sore, if it is rubbed off.

Prompt treatment is required to stop its progress, and tobacco-water rubbed into the skin is a good application, or dipping the sheep in a solution of arsenic, which also contains some sulphur, is effectual ; or an ointment rubbed into the skin is found to answer, composed of the following (rubbed into the skin in lines about four inches apart) :—

Hog's lard...	2 lbs.
Oil of tar	½ lb.
Sulphur	1 lb.

These remedies should be applied whenever scab is even only suspected, as a precautionary measure.

85. **TURN-SICK, GIDDINESS.**—Called in various localities

Goggles, Sturdy-gig, Dunt, Staggers, and Blob-whirl, is due to the presence of one or more hydatids on the brain, the sheep mostly attacked by it being those under two years of age. As before described, trepanning has been attempted with more or less success, but it is not to be depended upon.

86. **INFLAMMATION OF THE BRAIN (PHRENITIS).**—Excess of nourishment is mostly the cause of inflammation of the brain with sheep; but the disorder is not of a very common occurrence, mostly taking place when they have been suddenly removed from poor food and put upon rich. The disease sometimes causes the animal to display great violence, quite opposed to the usual quiet demeanour of a sheep; and the jugular vein should be at once opened, and from 8 ozs. to 1 lb. of blood abstracted, and a purgative given, consisting of 2 ozs. of sulphate of magnesia. In the case of a lamb, a smaller dose should be given, and less blood abstracted in proportion.

87. **PALSY.**—Palsy is produced by excessive cold and moisture, lambs being more subject to it than sheep, the loins being most generally affected, a suspension of the powers of the nervous system taking place. An excessive quantity of cold roots has been known to produce it—warmth of the animal economy being the best restorative. A stimulant of a suitable nature can be composed of the following ingredients :—

Powdered ginger..............................	1 drachm.
Powdered gentian	1 ,,
Spirit of nitrous ether	1 ,,

Administered twice a-day to a sheep, and from a quarter to half the quantity to a lamb.

88. **APOPLEXY.**—Must be treated in the same way as prescribed for inflammation of the brain, being a sudden determination of blood to the head.

89. **INFLAMMATION OF THE BLADDER.** — Rams are more liable to this disorder than ewes, which frequently results from high feeding, and when supplied with such highly nutritious food as beans and oil-cake, when the internal coat of the bladder becomes inflamed.

Bleeding from the neck should be resorted to, and aperient medicine and opiates given. Injections of warm water or linseed-tea are sometimes administered, mixed with small doses of laudanum.

90. **AILMENTS OF THE UDDER.** — After the lambs have

been taken away from the ewes, their udders are not unfrequently affected by tumours, which, if not attended to, sometimes end in mortification. Preventive means can, however, be taken to guard against this happening, by milking the ewes a few times after weaning. If this is neglected, and a curing process is necessary, the part affected should be frequently rubbed with camphorated spirits of wine. If the tumours suppurate, they should be opened with a sharp penknife, and the wound so caused cured by a healing salve.

91. **SORE TEATS.**—When the ewes have sore teats they will sometimes refuse to allow the lambs to suck. The lamb, in such a case, should be put to another ewe—which, although sometimes difficult to manage, may be done by using certain means—or fed by hand with cows'-milk, or milk taken by hand from the ewe. The udder should be bathed in warm water for some time, and afterwards washed with goulard water, spirits, or a slight infusion of sugar of lead. These, carefully repeated, will generally effect a cure; but if not, and there is much inflammation, the teats should be poulticed, to cause suppuration.

92. **DISEASES PECULIAR TO EWES.**—Slipping the lamb is generally occasioned by the animals being hard-driven, or worried by dogs, or hunted about when heavy with young; or by being cast into ruts, where they struggle violently in their attempts to rise. It is said, also, that when ewes are fed upon rape, it is apt to be produced.

Protrusion of the uterus usually takes place after an ewe has had a difficult labour, when it should be returned as quickly as possible, and means taken to confine it in its proper position, which may be done by putting a ring through the lips of the orifice, the same as are used for ringing swine; or a narrow strip of lead, twisted at the ends to secure it, which is found to answer the purpose very well.

SHEEP FOLDING HURDLE WITH LAMB CREEP.

CHAPTER VII.

IN THE MARKET.

Fattening Sheep—Markets—Selection for Market—Treatment on the Road—
Sending by Rail—Slaughtering—Imports of Sheep—Profits resulting from
Sheep-farming.

93. **FATTENING SHEEP.**—Sheep can be made fat through a
great variety of different ways of feeding, but of course the main
object is to do this in the most economical manner, and also in
the shortest space of time.

Corn, doubtless, is a most effective agent in fattening all animals,
the drawback to its use being the expense; so that grain can
seldom be given profitably to sheep in its entirety, though meal of
various kinds can be used economically in conjunction with roots.

Nothing, perhaps, has proved of greater assistance in fattening
sheep than oil-cake, for when fed upon turnips the addition of 1 lb.
of oil-cake per day will make a wonderful difference in the rapidity
of the progress and general health.

Hay or straw should always be given to promote digestion, the
most effectual manner being in the form of chaff, whether they are
fed upon mangold-wurzel, cabbages, turnips, swedes or carrots.

Many sheep are fattened without the admixture of any other
than natural food, upon rich grazing grounds, where they arrive
gradually at a state of perfection; though it is not every kind of
pasture that is capable of fattening sheep, and on these it will be
found desirable to use concentrated food in some form or other in
addition.

A certain degree of fatness is absolutely necessary, but when
carried too far it does not pay the feeder, tending more to increase
of tallow than advantage to the mutton. The quantity of inside fat
depends a good deal upon the age and time of fattening, old sheep
making more than young ones; the tallow of a wether in the ordi-

nary way of feeding averaging from an eighth to a tenth of its dead weight.

94. **MARKETS.**—The markets for sheep are very numerous, there scarcely being a county town of any size without its sheep and cattle-market; though some of the great fairs, as Weyhill Fair, attract great numbers of sheep, and a very large amount of business is done in them.

95. **SELECTION FOR MARKET.**—In pursuing a definite system of management, in order to ensure the highest state of effibiency of a flock, a system of continued selection should be carried on, and all indifferent animals weeded out and sent to market.

Old ewes should be replaced by an equal number of the best and most vigorous female lambs; in well-managed sheep-farms in .the southern counties of England, this process of selection being generally carried out from six to ten weeks after shearing-time.

Not only is this selection necessary for weeding out the faulty specimens arising from either defects or old age—for the purpose of sending them to market, and selling them off—but they should be separated, and assigned to different pastures according to their strength or weakness; placing those animals that are designed for fattening in one place, the ewes by themselves and the wethers also in the same way; the two-year-old in one parcel, and the old wethers and rams in another; and, lastly, the lambs by themselves; other-wise the stronger will injure the weaker animals, and eat up the best food which the weakest have the most pressing need of.

96. **TREATMENT ON THE ROAD.**—We have incidentally spoken before of the evils attendant upon over-driving, and this part of the business should be carefully managed, and if the animals have to travel a long distance, arrangements should be made beforehand for their reception on the journey where they can be turned upon accommodation land, which is generally to be obtained without much difficulty.

97. **SENDING BY RAIL.**—The long journeys, however, which used to be painfully performed by large droves of cattle, and flocks of sheep, along dusty high roads, when the animals suffered greatly from thirst and heat, have been superseded in a great measure by railway travelling, the legislature having issued certain regulations which are under the control of the Privy Council, for the proper conveyance of all animals. And not only the pens in which they are kept, but the trucks in which they are conveyed, are regularly white-washed, and every precaution is taken to ensure against contagion

and other incidental evils that at one time were rife ; so that on this account there is very little room for sheep-farmers to complain, though there were so many complaints at one time of the barbarity often exercised, that an Act was passed, 3 Geo. IV., c. 71, s. 1, which contained the proviso that any persons wantonly ill-treating any species of cattle, may be summoned before any Justice of the Peace, and, if convicted upon oath, are subject to a penalty according to circumstances, not under 10s. nor above £5, or in default of pay-ment, to be committed to the House of Correction for any period not exceeding three months.

98. SLAUGHTERING.—Sheep are quickly and easily slaughtered, being generally stuck in the neck, and hung up with their heads downwards; but as the services of an experienced butcher are always to be obtained for a trifle, and it is much the best way for a farmer to avail himself of them, a detailed description of the method of slaughtering sheep is scarcely necessary.

99. IMPORTS OF SHEEP.—A good many sheep are imported into England from various parts of the Continent, the supply ever fluctuating according to the condition of our markets here. Stringent rules are now in vogue against contagion, and all infected animals are at once slaughtered at the place of debarkation.

100. PROFITS RESULTING FROM SHEEP-FARMING.—It is very difficult to give any definite account of the profits to be obtained by sheep-farming, as there are so many indirect advantages to be obtained in connection with it, in addition to and beyond the mere debtor and creditor account; such as the opportunity of manuring the land through this means, and the conversion of bulky, heavy crops of comparatively small value, into so much portable wool and mutton, for which there is always a ready market at one's doors, as it may be said.

With skilful management, however, as mutton realises a high price, sheep-farming can be made very remunerative ; particularly if all waste is avoided in feeding, and full use is made of those economical contrivances for cking out the food of the farm which have been already glanced at. It may safely be affirmed, that by skilful management in the matter of feeding, and all other depart-ments equally well looked after, that a-saving in the cost of fodder may be gained which will amount to one-third less than the expense incurred by careless sheep-farmers, who permit a large amount of waste—though, perhaps, not knowingly—to take place every day in the management of their stock.

A Good Breed.

CHAPTER VIII.

PIGS.

Natural History of the Hog—Varieties—Foreign Breeds—French Pigs—Prussian or Polish Pigs—Spanish Pigs—German Pigs—British Breeds—The Berkshire —Improved Essex Pig—The Suffolk and Norfolk—The Cheshire Pig—The Old Lincolnshire, or Yorkshire Pig—The Improved Lincolnshire Pig—The Small Breed, or Prick-eared Lincolnshire—The Old Irish—The Rudgewick— The Hampshire Hog—The Shropshire—The Gloucester—The Chinese—The Mediterranean Breeds—Scotch Pigs—The " Tunkey " or Tonquin.

101. **THE NATURAL HISTORY OF THE HOG.**—The hog is found in a wild state in several European and Asiatic countries; and though boar-hunting is not now practised in England, yet, before the land was enclosed, many wild hogs were to be found and the pastime was carried on in these islands, but never to a very great extent. The latest resemblance to the wild boar that has been seen in modern times in Britain was the old Highland breed of pig, which has been described as an ugly little brindled monster, scarcely bigger than an English terrier.

Wild pigs are found in the distant islands of the Pacific, as well as other places far out of the usual track of ordinary voyagers; but these, in many instances, have originally sprung from pigs that have been put ashore by voyagers.

In India they are found in large numbers, and there "pig-sticking" is a very popular sport; and the race known as the Chinese pig is supposed to have come to us from the Indies, of which there are two distinct species—the white and the black; the former the better-shaped animals of the two, but not so hardy or so prolific as the latter—the black being thrifty, and fattening upon a comparatively small quantity of food.

Some writers are of opinion that to the Chinese pig, and to the pigs that have been introduced from the shores of the Mediterranean, we are indebted for the greatly-improved race of swine that now figure so prominently in all English farm-yards; the sleek, contented animals in the condition they are now mostly seen offering a very distinct contrast to the old wild boar, the actual denizen of the forest, when—

> "His bristled back a trench impaled appears,
> And stands erected like a field of spears."

In his wild state, the animal is both herbivorous and carnivorous to a certain extent, eating frogs, field-mice, sedge in miry grounds, fern, and the wild fruits and berries that fall from the trees to the ground, still keeping up their universal appetite in their tame condition, nothing coming amiss to them, and feeding on sloes, crabs, "hips and haws," beech-mast, acorns and similar products. As to their habit of turning up the earth in search of roots of all kinds with their snouts—a trait which they still retain, and which many a ploughed-up piece of pasture-land has borne witness to where pigs have obtained access, and they have not been properly "ringed"— it may be remarked here, that if the gristle in the tops of the snouts of young pigs is cut off with a razor, they are rendered incapable of the destructive turning up the ground which they often practise, ploughing up the turf in long stretches, which is both unsightly and detrimental—the place healing over while they are young, without very much trouble.

Of the acute sense of smell possessed by the pig, Rowlandson remarks that—"The acuteness of its olfactory organs has been made subservient to the uses of man by the truffle-hunter. This faculty has also been made use of in setting game in the two well-known instances of Colonel Thornton, and the sow now broken in by Mr. Foomer, gamekeeper to Sir H. P. St. John Mildmay. In both instances, it was remarked that the scent of the game was noticed by the pig when it had been passed over by the best pointers."

The consumption of pork and bacon is very large in Great

Britain, but the price realised by the farmer is kept down by the immense importations that now take place from America, where the "hog-crop," as it is termed, is very large each year.

As it principally comes to us in the form of bacon, or pickled pork (the latter of which, upon occasions of glut, has been sold as low as 2½d. per pound in Liverpool), there is not that competition to be feared in the case of "porker pigs," or pigs of a small size that are sold by pork-butchers, who get a long price for choice meat. There can be no doubt the omnivorous appetite of the pig is not turned to such good account as it might often be made to do by English farmers, in resorting to many economical contrivances in feeding, that are often entirely overlooked, which will be glanced at in the pages that follow.

Indeed, it will be upon a much greater resort to economical feeding and management of stock, that the profits of the future English farmer will be made to depend. Pigs have long been regarded as useful stock that eat up refuse, or damaged produce of varied kinds, which otherwise would become entirely wasted; but the principle may be carried to a much further extent than most farmers in this country ever dream of carrying it, and enormous quantities of *weeds* that are collected in our fields could be made to come in as food for store-stock, supplemented by other of a better condition, if collected and thrown over into their sties from time to time.

What the pigs did not eat in this way, their hooves would convert into valuable manure, of which few farmers can obtain enough.

The pig is often spoken of as an animal of proverbially filthy habits. It is true that he will wallow in the mire, but this does not arise from an inherent love of filth—for the pig can relish a delicate morsel with as lively an appreciation as any known animal, and perhaps enjoy it with more real *gusto*—but feeding often upon food of a very heating description, he rolls in miry places simply to *cool his skin.*

Pigs that have been fed upon beans, peas, and other heating food often have sores break out at the back of their ears, which speaks plainly of the heated condition of their bodies; and can it be wondered at, that the poor animals under such circumstances wallow in cool places, although they are miry? Pigs will be found to thrive best when they are kept very clean, and an occasional washing even proves of infinite service to them. The manure they produce is very valuable, the quality being only inferior to that of the sheep.

102. **VARIETIES.**—There are numerous varieties of pigs, the old English breed, that used at one time to possess strongly-marked individual characteristics, being gradually improved away, and more profitable breeds substituted in their places, which better answers the purpose of the farmer.

For ordinary purposes, the improved Berkshire breed stands the highest in general estimation; the most marked varieties that find favour in various districts, that are kept, perhaps, because they are either met with most commonly in those particular districts, or are found to answer best the special objects of each breeder, or storekeeper, being the Chinese, Essex, Suffolk and Norfolk, Shropshire, Hampshire, Woburn, Dishly, and Rudgewick, besides the original English breeds, to which we shall make cursory allusion.

183. FOREIGN BREEDS.—Of the various foreign breeds of pigs it will be only worth while mentioning for practical purposes, besides the Chinese pigs above referred to, the Neapolitan, Maltese, and similar breeds of pigs that have come to us from the shores of the Mediterranean; as from these it is supposed the English breeds of pigs owe much of their improvement, so far as the small varieties are concerned. More especially the black kinds, to which they are indebted for their improved delicacy of flesh and beauty of form, fineness of bone, round plump shape, fine snout, and soft hair and bristle, resulting from a finer skin (a change in the latter particular being only regretted by the brushmaker); many of them being almost without hair or bristle, their aptitude to fatten at an early age being unequalled, and the flavour of the meat unsurpassed where delicacy is sought for, and not the large bacon upon which farm-labourers at one time used chiefly to be fed, when they lived in the house with the farmer's family.

104. FRENCH PIGS.—French pigs are, for the most part, tall, thin and coarse, though of late years more attention has been paid to improvement of breed than at one time was the case, pork not being held in so much estimation by our neighbours across the Channel, whose culinary tastes more accord with stews that are produced from the gravy of meats of a different order, which they consume with large quantities of vegetables; from whom the English lower classes might with great advantage take a useful lesson, in the establishment of the universal stew-pot.

105. PRUSSIAN OR POLISH PIGS.—Prussian or Polish pigs are mostly large in size, and coarse; and are both bad breeders and bad feeders.

106. THE SPANISH PIG.—Spanish pigs are small in size, and not particularly noteworthy beyond being of good flavour, and making capital sweet meat; which is supposed to be owing, in many instances, to their being largely fed upon the sweet chestnut, of which great quantities are grown in Spain.

107. **GERMAN PIGS.**—German pigs are smaller than the Prussian, or Podolian, but are better feeders; the Bavarian pigs being still smaller in size.

108. **BRITISH BREEDS.**—Most of the British breeds of pigs possess distinctive peculiarities of their own, which are more specially adapted to the objects in view entertained by different people, and thus some farmers require a larger, stronger, and hardier race than others, to suit their own particular purpose; some pigs being contented with rough food, while others require provision of a more delicate quality. The dairyman, or dairy-

BERKSHIRE PIG.

farmer, that has a large quantity of skimmed milk to spare, the refuse of butter-making, will find his greatest profit in rearing the small breeds, that fatten quickly and can be sold as "porkers," which fetch a long price from the best pork-butchers; while farmers who have a lot of coarse or spoiled food to be eaten up, will find their account in a larger and hardier race.

109. **THE BERKSHIRE.**—The *improved* Berkshire breed is perhaps the best of all the English breeds of pigs for general purposes, but it has been crossed so often with other varieties, that it is often presented under somewhat different aspects; but the cross with the Tonquin, or "Tunkey" pigs, as they are sometimes called, has resulted in producing a very superior race, being black and white, short-haired, fine-skinned, and with smaller heads and ears than

the Berkshire, some of them having quite pointed or "prick" ears, feathered with hair inside, which is a distinctive mark of both; very fine in bone; broad and deep in the belly; full hind quarters; and light in offal. Such breeds, founded upon the Berkshire old stock, wear different names, and form, as it were distinctive breeds, as "Essex Half-blacks," "Essex and Hertford Breed;" the hardihood of the original Berkshire, which is retained in many of these new *improved* breeds, being a leading and most valuable feature.

Loudon describes the old Berkshire pig as "being in general of a tawny white, or reddish colour, spotted with black; large ears hanging over the eyes; thick, close, and well-made in body; legs short; small in the bone; having a disposition to fatten quickly, and, when well fed, the flesh is fine; feeds to a great weight; is good for either pork or bacon."

Another description of the Berkshire hog accredits it as being of a reddish-brown colour with black spots, well-placed head, but with large ears, sometimes hanging over the eyes and sometimes standing forward, being short-legged, small-boned, and of a rough, curly coat, to all appearance indicating flesh of a coarse quality, though nothing can be finer than the bacon, the hogs attaining to a great size, sometimes reaching the weight of 100 stones, but 40 or 50 stones when fattened being the more common average.

Such, doubtless, was a fair description of the old Berkshire, but of late their size has been reduced, and instead of the rough yellowish, or tawny coat—although vestiges of it remain in many instances—they are mostly black and white, and often nearly black, the latter including the hardiest breeds, while the whiter colours partake more largely of the Chinese cross.

The black, or black-and-white breeds of medium size, are perhaps the best stock that can be kept. They are hardy, not susceptible to changes of the weather, as some of the more delicate breeds of pigs are, will eat almost anything, and do well upon rough fare—a most important consideration in pig-keeping—and fatten quickly when put upon good food; they are fairly prolific, though they do not bring such large litters as some other breeds that can be mentioned.

110. **IMPROVED ESSEX PIG.**—These, originally descendants of the Berkshire, located in Essex, crossed with Chinese and black Neapolitan, have resulted in a very superior breed, which takes equal rank perhaps with the improved Berkshire. The old breed has been described as "up-eared with long sharp heads; roach-backed; carcases flat, long, and general'y high upon the head;

bone not large; colour white, or black-and-white; bare of hair; quick feeders, but great consumers; and of an unquiet disposition." This not very flattering picture has been succeeded by the improved breed alluded to.

111. **THE SUFFOLK AND NORFOLK.**—These have been held in high estimation as a useful and prolific race, though not of very large size; lately they have been crossed to a very considerable extent by the Berkshire—the improved Berkshire pig occupying much the same relative position amongst swine as the improved Leicester does among sheep.

:ESSEX PIG.

112. **THE CHESHIRE PIG.**—The old Cheshire pig formerly attained an enormous size, some individual specimens almost equalling the proportions of a bullock.

Culley in his " Observations on Live Stock," says :—

" On Monday the 24th January, 1774, a pig (fed by Mr. Joseph Lawson, of Cheshire) was killed, which measured, from the nose to the end of the tail, three yards eight inches, and in height four feet five inches and a half; when alive it weighed 12 cwt., 2 qrs., 10 lbs., or 86 stone, 10 lbs. avoirdupois. This pig was killed by James Washington, butcher, Congleton in Cheshire."

The name of the butcher which is given, may be presumed to be furnished not on account of his having the honour of killing so large a pig, but by way of evidence or attestation of the fact narrated.

The old breed are described as standing very high on long legs, having large heads, with long hanging ears, narrow back greatly curved, with deep flat sides varying in colour, being white, blue-and-white, black-and-white.

113. **THE OLD LINCOLNSHIRE, OR YORKSHIRE PIG.**—The old Lincolnshire, or Yorkshire pig, was of very large size, extremely long in the leg, and weak-loined, being very long-bodied, with long, coarse, curly hair; the flesh being flabby and of inferior quality.

114. **THE IMPROVED LINCOLNSHIRE PIG.**—Upon the un-promising materials described above have been grafted the *improved* breed, of which there may be said to be two varieties—the large breed, or wold pig, which is mostly met with in the Lincolnshire wolds, and throughout a large portion of the county of York, and the counties bordering on Lancashire; and the small breed, or pointed prick-eared pig, which are chiefly met with in the more southern parts of the county, and the adjoining ones of Northamptonshire, Leicestershire, Huntingdonshire, and Cambridgeshire.

The original large breed has been almost displaced, the race occupying its place being very much improved, with far better points; such as broad back, with wide, well-set rump, springing ribs, and broad chine and loin, with deep sides, and full chest.

It is generally considered a profitable kind of pig; feeding well, and growing fast, attaining 20 to 25 imperial stones, in twelve months from birth when well fed, the pork being remarkably good, and possessing a full proportion of fine lean flesh.

115. **THE SMALL BREED; OR, PRICK-EARED LINCOLN-SHIRE.**—These are not the small animals which their names would describe, as they are as fine a race of pigs as can be found; but the term probably grew up in distinguishing them from the old Lin-colnshire, which was one of the largest breeds in the kingdom—clever breeders having attained the object of securing the desirable points of the smaller races which they have grafted upon a large frame, reaching maturity early, and being compactly formed, broad-chested, and accompanied with lightness of offal.

116. **THE OLD IRISH.**—While speaking of large-sized pigs, we must not forget to mention here the old Irish, which Parkinson says "are all of the size of a large jackass, and very large-boned, and being of such an unprofitable nature that it is not uncommon for the poorer sort of men to be two years in fattening a pig."

Large mis-shapen animals with long, hanging ears, strong bristly hair, and narrow frame—their colours were various, being white, black-and-white, and spotted. But of late years, by judicious cross-ing—mostly with Berkshire and some of the smaller breeds, as Suffolk and Norfolk—they have become vastly improved, and Irish bacon, which at one time was considered inferior, now occupies a high place in the market, a good deal of it finding its way to London.

117. **THE RUDGEWICK.**—This breed of pig, though long known and reared on the borders of Sussex and Surrey, and celebrated for their extraordinary size, appears to have been a good deal con-fined to the district mentioned, some of them attaining to the weight of oxen, instances being recorded in some of the County Reports of enormous weights having been reached, individual examples being quoted of 91 stone, 93 stone, 99 stone, and 116 stone; while the almost incredible weight of 182 stone was reached in one instance, at three years old! These weights must cause them to be considered the largest kind in Britain, but this very large-sized pork and bacon is now no longer marketable, as once was the case; which in all probability is the reason why we hear so little of the breed that was once so celebrated.

118. **THE HAMPSHIRE HOG.**—The Hampshire bacon has long been celebrated, but it is supposed to have been caused by the fact of its being fed when young to a great extent upon the mast that is to be found in the New Forest, and to the capital method of curing it, rather than to any inherent good qualities of the breed itself; being somewhat of a coarse animal, though fattening easily. But, in common with most other original breeds, it is now seldom met with as a pure race, having been largely crossed with the Berkshire, Chinese, Suffolk, and other breeds. These judicious crossings have resulted in an animal that is not only naturally hardy, but one that can be fattened at an early age, unlike some other breeds that must be kept for a considerable time as store pigs before the fattening process is commenced. The original breed was never of an extremely large size.

119. **THE SHROPSHIRE.**—The Shropshire is a somewhat large-sized pig, the prevailing colour being white or brindled, but pos-sessing no very salient features.

120. **THE GLOUCESTER.**—The Gloucester is somewhat remark-able, on account of its having two wattle-like appendages hanging from the throat. It is not a well-formed or compact race, and does not call for any particular mention beyond the peculiarity referred to.

G

121. **THE CHINESE.**—What are termed the pure Chinese breed, though raised and naturalised in England, are beautifully white, both as regards the skin and the hair; the former being remarkably thin, and the latter thinly set with a few fine bristles; the snout being rather broad; head short; eyes bright and fiery; very small prick ears; wide cheek: high chine; and disproportionately large neck, which seems to be one with the carcase, when fat, so as to be without shape or symmetry. The legs are remarkably short, the belly nearly touching the ground; with an unusually short tail.

The flesh is delicate when fed upon the best food, as barley-meal and skimmed milk; but becomes oily and fat if the animal is fed

CHINESE PIG.

with animal or greasy substances; for it will eat almost anything, its prevailing tendency being to make fat; the cross with the English breeds having reduced this tendency. When fattened, there is scarcely any useless offal to be dealt with.

There are, however, many varieties of distinct kinds, at least seven kinds of Chinese being classified, difference in colour and size forming the chief variations. The small white breed is considered to be almost perfection in its shape and leading characteristics. Parkinson describes them as "being pigs in miniature; their legs about two-and-a-half inches long; ears about the size of a large leaf on an apple-tree; the length of the jaw, from the snout to the crown, about six inches; from the crown to where the tail is set on, about two feet; height about twelve inches; weight, when full-grown and fat, six stones at two years old." They are some-what delicate. The Black Chinese with bald faces, which possess something of the same bodily characteristics, are at once hardier, grow quicker, and are more prolific and reach heavier weights when fat.

The large black breed are the largest of all the Chinese varieties, being beautifully-shaped pigs, and reaching heavy weights when well fed; thirty stone being attained, and sometimes as much as forty, though the latter is a very unusual weight for this kind of pig.

122. **THE MEDITERRANEAN BREEDS.**—The Mediterranean breeds, including the Maltese and Neapolitan, to which we have alluded before, are round, plump and symmetrical; satisfying to the eye of the best judges, being shorter in body than the Chinese, but, upon the whole, somewhat larger in frame, being coal-black and almost entirely without hair or bristles. The most noticeable feature in connection with this race of pigs is their aptitude to fatten at an early age, and the pork produced by them is of very fine quality. They are tolerably prolific, and will thrive pretty well upon only moderate food; but there are many better breeds, as the improved Berkshire, which will answer the ordinary farmer's purpose better to keep, though all the breeds of this nature, as well as the Chinese, are admirably adapted, as before said, for the dairy-farmer.

123. **SCOTCH PIGS.**—The Scotch breeds of pigs were various, and of different varieties, but all of a very inferior description, until an improvement took place by crossing with English pigs.

124. **THE "TUNKEY," OR TONQUIN.**—This variety, alluded to before, is a small race, which make very delicate pork, and fatten early, being mostly white, of thick compact shape. They are fine-boned and short in the leg, attaining good weights in comparison to their size, and are of the kind most approved when sold in the form of small pork, and are therefore better adapted for the purpose of the dairyman than the farmer.

The foregoing list includes all the most noticeable breeds of pigs. There are other distinct races, such as the Herefordshire and the Wiltshire, but they do not call for any particular mention or notice; but, as we proceed, we shall duly point out the kind of breed best suited for certain definite ends, as the farmer should make choice of a race of pigs in accordance with his means and opportunities of keeping them to the best advantage.

CUMBERLAND PIG.

CHAPTER IX.

PIGS (*continued*).

Names of Pigs—Statistics relating to Hogs in the United Kingdom, Australia, and America—Characteristics of a good Boar and Sow—Uses—As Food.

125. **NAMES OF PIGS.**—Pigs are known by different names and terms, according to their age, sex, and condition. The female is called a sow; when spayed, a gelt or sow-pig—the operation of spaying being performed when the young sows are intended to be sold off fattened, or as store-pigs; the male being called a boar, or brawn, and when castrated a gelt, or cut-pig, hog-pig, or barrow-pig—in different stages of their growth and condition. The general terms applied to both sexes are: sucklers, fatting-pigs, and store-pigs; and the whole race is spoken of collectively as swine, hogs, or pigs indifferently.

126. **STATISTICS RELATING TO HOGS IN THE UNITED KINGDOM, AUSTRALIA, AND AMERICA.**— According to the Agricultural Returns of Live Stock issued by the Government in October, 1879, pigs in Great Britain were fewer in number by nearly 16 per cent. than in the year 1878. The competition of American bacon is reported to have reduced the price of pork and bacon, and a species of typhoid is also noticed by some collectors, especially in the south of England, as accounting for a great part of the decrease. There is also a proportionate reduction in the number of pigs in Ireland.

It may also be incidentally mentioned here that the number of pigs in Australia were given in the same report as 815,000; while the report received by the Department of Agriculture at Washington states that the number of pigs in the United States amounted to 34¾ millions.

127. CHARACTERISTICS OF A GOOD BOAR AND SOW. — As will be seen from the description given of the various breeds of pigs, the points of the different races vary a good deal, but there are certain good qualities that are common to all, the characteristic signs of a good hog being moderate length as to the carcase, the head and cheek being plump and full, the neck short and thick; fine bone; full quarters; the proportions of the whole body being in accordance with the symmetry proper to each respective breed or variety.

In choosing a boar much depends upon local prejudice, so that it is somewhat hard to lay down a general rule, but a large-headed animal should be avoided, and one selected that is deep and broad in the chest, chine rather arched, with ribs and barrel well rounded, and his haunch falling full down nearly to the hock.

The boar should be more compact in his form, and rather smaller than the sow, because if the latter is somewhat coarse her offspring will be improved by the cross in form and flesh, and the more roomy she is, the greater likelihood of her producing a numerous and healthy litter.

The sow on this account should be chosen with a deep and capacious belly, and as symmetrical in proportion as the character of her breed will allow. One important point is that she has at least ten or a dozen teats; for as each sucking pig attaches itself to one particular teat, if there be not enough to tally with the number of pigs given birth to, some little outcast or other can only obtain a scanty allowance when the others fall off here and there, and will in consequence go back in condition.

128. USES.—The chief uses of the pig consist in its marketable value as food for man, and as a manufacturer of valuable manure on a farm; in England, the bristles and skin being only of very secondary importance. Bristles are used in the manufacture of brushes, and for other subsidiary purposes, while the skin makes excellent saddles, bags, &c., but these are chiefly sent to us from abroad, and are taken very little account of by the ordinary English agriculturist; the bristles being mostly burnt, or scraped off when the pig is killed, the skin being left upon the meat, which helps to

preserve it in the form of bacon and hams, and in this form, and that of fresh pork, which becomes "crackling" when roasted.

129. AS FOOD.—Buffon has pointed out that the fat of man, and of those animals which have no suet, as the dog and horse, are pretty equally mixed with the flesh, while the suet of the sheep, goat, and deer is found only at its extremities; but the fat of the hog covers the animal all over, and forms a thick, distinct, and continued layer between the flesh and the skin, thus differing from that of every other quadruped.

The drying of hams and bacon is very easily performed, it being usual in old times to hang them up in the wide kitchen chimneys of the old-fashioned farm-houses, where wood used formerly to be chiefly burnt for fuel. But proper smoke-houses can be constructed for a very trifling sum, made of a few boards, about 7 feet high, closed on all sides, with a small hole in the roof for the smoke to escape through. Saw-dust should be spread all over the earthen floor, to about the depth of 5 or 6 inches, which, when kindled, will smoulder without breaking out into flame. Pieces of timber, strong enough to bear the weight of the flitches and hams, should be placed across, so that the ends of the flitches hang down within a couple of feet or more of the floor, the neck being downwards. It is of no consequence how closely they hang together, so that they do not absolutely touch one another.

Generally speaking, they will be cured in this way in about a fortnight's time, the hams requiring longer.

The flavour of the hams is considerably improved if sugar is used in curing, in the proportion of 1 lb. of sugar to 3 lbs. of salt, and 2 ozs. of saltpetre. The sugar not only assists in preserving the meat, but renders its fibres mellow, while it corrects the extreme pungency that is often given to the flavour of bacon and hams by the too liberal use of salt alone.

In some parts of the Continent the hide is stripped off, under the belief that the flesh takes the salt better, and the hide is sold to saddlers for making saddles, but the practice is hardly ever followed in England.

When the farmer is in a position to feed his pigs and make them fat as porkers, in the event of his carrying on dairying operations, or having means at his command to feed his pigs advantageously, it is found very profitable to sell off his produce in the shape of young pork. But when his object is to keep store pigs to eat up any rough food that he may have to dispose of, such as diseased potatoes, vegetables, or various farm refuse, he must necessarily keep them a certain time, and then sell them alive, or fatten them off for bacon; for in the shape of pickled pork, he cannot compete with barrelled pork that is imported.

YORKSHIRE PIG.

CHAPTER X.

PIGS (*continued*).

Management of Stock—Feeding—Fattening—Ringing—Slaughtering—Pig-styes
and Piggeries—Breeding—Period of Gestation—Sows Destroying their Young
—Littering Sows—Rearing—Sucking Pigs—Weaning.

130. **MANAGEMENT OF STOCK.**—There are several ways of
profitably managing swine, which must depend a good deal upon
the capabilities of the farm, or situation occupied by the breeder
or stock-keeper; for many people do not take the trouble to breed
pigs themselves, but merely buy in young animals to eat up a certain amount of food that otherwise would be wasted, but which these
animals glean, and then sell them off afterwards fattened.

Store-pigs, which had attained half their growth, used formerly
to be separated from the others in the course of the month of May,
and turned into the fields, where they were kept till Michaelmas,
the gates being closed upon them, and care being taken that the
fences were in sound condition, so that they did not break out and
wander to some other points where they might do a considerable
amount of damage in a very short time. But this plan, although
partially carried out, on account of the different system of farming
which now most commonly prevails, and the reduced amount of
fallow land there is, is not so frequently resorted to; and now they
are not turned out so much, except towards autumn, when they are
put upon the stubbles and other spots, where they are enabled

to pick up a tolerably good living for themselves without any great amount of cost having to be incurred. Still, under a good course of management, and by methods of feeding not generally practised, pigs can be kept upon a farm for a comparatively much smaller amount than their food usually costs, if not in absolute money, which cannot be actually reckoned, in the amount of good food consumed, of which we will briefly speak.

131. **FEEDING.**—The custom of turning pigs out is indeed a very good and profitable one at certain seasons of the year ; but it is not at times nearly so advantageous as keeping them in their styes (where their manure accumulates) and carrying their food to them.

The profitable time for turning swine out is, as before-mentioned, after harvest, when they can pick up a good deal amongst the stubbles, and eat the springing clover or other grasses, and especially where there are oak trees, either in woods or plantations, or placed round the fields as hedge-row timber, as well as where beech-mast is to be found.

Some oak trees will produce a very large quantity of acorns, which fall day by day, and the pigs, where these abound, may be seen making their daily rounds from tree to tree, and scampering off to another tree as soon as all the acorns beneath one are picked up.

Pigs will eat a good deal of grass, and find both health and amusement from being turned into a meadow, but their manure is then dropped about, and not concentrated in one spot, with the addition of much other matter which can be added to swell up the manure-heap, and it is when the pig-stye is regarded as a manufactory of manure upon a large scale, that pigs become so valuable to the farmer; though swine can be kept profitably by resorting to economical contrivances, and be made to answer well, even without looking upon the manure as the chief source of profit, which is the light in which many farmers are in the habit of regarding the subject.

They, however, cannot be made to do this as store-pigs between the ages of two months and twelve months old, which is the most unprofitable time in the life of a pig that is kept as a store animal, though breeding sows can be made eminently profitable. If the farmer has no skimmed milk, or spoiled grain with which to fatten young pigs and sell them off as porkers, if he breeds upon a large scale it will be found to pay best to sell the young pigs off directly they are weaned. If he wants the manure, and can find any kind of rough food—and there are many sources which will supply this that are very often overlooked—store-pigs will answer his purpose to keep, but not without.

Although it never answers the purpose to have any animal in a half-starved condition, which is the most expensive possible way of keeping stock in the long run, yet, as pigs of a hardy breed, as the Berkshire, are coarse feeders, there is a vast amount of possible fodder that is often entirely neglected, that may be used to great advantage.

Where any number of pigs are kept, there ought to be two distinct sets of cooking-apparatus: a good large copper for boiling, and a small kind of *kiln* for baking. The latter can be constructed at a trifling expense, and should consist of a few bricks built up to support a thick, flat plate of iron, beneath which is a fire-hole, and so make a rough kind of oven, but more open than an oven, and partaking rather of the nature of a *kiln*.

Upon this sheet of iron, which will constitute the chief expense, and may possibly cost a pound, diseased potatoes may be *baked*. Unfortunately, since the potato disease has become established in this country, there is no lack of diseased potatoes, either of one's own growing, or that can be purchased of one's neighbours ; and some of these are in a deplorable condition, and as the longer they are kept the worse they get, till they sometimes become an offensive, pasty mass, instead of boiling them, and stamping them down in barrels, or in a pit, and sprinkling salt over them—both excellent ways of preserving diseased or other potatoes for food—the baking process will be found a capital one, the undue moisture in the diseased part being dried up, and the whole made so palatable that pigs will eat them as readily as they will do corn.

Diseased potatoes may often be bought for sixpence per bushel of farmers who want to get rid of them, and, when very bad, are sometimes sold for as little as threepence per bushel, people being often only too willing to get such offensive matter out of their way ; and as there are generally the result of sundry pickings over, and sortings, the supply is often pretty constant during the winter.

The kiln will often be found very useful for many other purposes, as when damp food needs to be dried ; and the firing can mostly be picked up and formed out of the trimmings of hedges, clumps of old wood, and odds and ends that lie about, and the ashes should be saved, and put in a dry place to drill in with seeds, or use as they may be wanted.

The copper should always be kept going, and all manner of refuse boiled up. Nettles which grow in hedges in too abundant pro-
fusion in many places, should all be gathered together by a lad with
a hook, and brought to the feeding-place for the use of the pigs. The
young ones will be eaten readily when green by the store-pigs, and
the older ones should be boiled, leaving out the very tough stalks.
These will boil up well with other green food, such as the outside
leaves of cabbages, or any refuse vegetables, and a few handfuls of
meal, pollard, or bran will vastly improve the quality of the mess,
and a large amount of food be got together at a very small cost.

The ordinary farm labourer will most likely deride the notion of
feeding pigs upon such food, and may not be found to enter very
readily into this kind of system, but those who have the feeding of
pigs should be made to do it.

In the north of England, the young tops of nettles are often eaten
and relished as a vegetable, and "nettle tea" is considered a very
fine thing for the blood in the spring of the year, and if good food
for man, it may safely be affirmed to be the same for pigs; and many
kinds of vegetable food that would not be eaten without being
cooked, when it finds its way to the copper, goes down very well
with the rest, and by boiling the rougher parts that would be rejected uncooked, these are softened and assimilated with the other.

When turnips are singled, or mangold, those that are cut out,
and the tops of early potatoes that are dug, should all be gathered
together and thrown down *outside* the pig-styes, and portions
thrown over several times during the course of the day. When
large quantities are thrown over at once, the pigs pick out some,
and in course of time trample down and spoil the remainder, before
they have time to consume a quarter of what might be eaten, had
it been thrown to them on separate occasions. When grass-plots
are mowed, or hedges trimmed, a similar course ought to be pursued, and the same with the vast quantities of weeds that often
come off the land in rainy seasons. These, instead of being burned
—a good enough practice of itself—should be carted to the pig-
styes, and served in the same way. Sow-thistle and other weeds
abound amongst it, and the earth attached to the roots will be
trodden down with that which is left, and their hooves will convert
the whole into a valuable manure; and when this is persistently
carried out, the amount that can be collected together where a
large number of pigs are kept will be enormous, and very much
surprise those who have never practised it.

Every farmer, or every person who has a large garden, has occasion to sweep up the leaves which fall in autumn, and make a clearance so that tidiness may prevail. These should all go to the pigs, to swell up the manure-heap, and amongst them will be acorns, beech-mast, and many unconsidered trifles that all swell up the amount of food for these hearty eaters to consume.

By such contrivances as these, the pigs' food-bill is kept down considerably, and, by resorting to them, even store-pigs may be kept almost without expense until they have attained to twelve months old, when, if put upon good food, they will be found to fatten readily, and be ready for the butcher upon a much smaller allowance of meal, or corn, than often would be supposed.

In following out a system of this kind, of course a hardy breed of pigs must be selected, such as the improved Berkshire.

When a number of cows are kept, or upon a dairy-farm where there is plenty of dairy-refuse, some of the smaller breeds that have been described, that reach a certain degree of maturity early, will be found the best class of pig to keep; but each person must, in this respect, be guided by his own circumstances.

Some farmers allow their store-pigs to graze over the clover and other artificial grasses. This, at best, is but a slovenly and wasteful practice, but is endeavoured to be justified sometimes by their owner pointing out that, when slaughtered, the pigs fetch a good round sum, and want but a few handfuls of corn whilst they are growing into money; but it will be readily seen that the method recommended is much more desirable and efficacious in carrying out the objects in view.

Brewers' grains make a good article of food for pigs, when they can be obtained cheap. They are sold at 1s. to 2s. per quarter by the large London brewers ; and, when pressed down in a pit, or a sugar hogshead, and kept for a few months, they undergo a kind of fermentation, and are much more serviceable to them on this account than when used fresh.

There is a dreadful outcry at the time these lines are being written, about agricultural distress and the unprofitable character of British agriculture; but the question may well be asked, Do English farmers rear their stock at the smallest possible rate of expense? Unfortunately they do not do this in many instances ; and unprofitable feeding, though not exactly to be called waste, in effect really amounts to much the same thing.

What would be thought of a manufacturer who put twice the amount of material into his fabrics that there was any real occasion for, or neglected his opportunities for economising the expenditure of his raw material ?

The large amount of food that an unprofitable breed of pig will consume is something enormous, especially if in lean or poor condition before the fattening process is begun ; cases being recorded where it has taken seventy-eight bushels of peas, barley, and oats to fatten one animal, which, however, was of large size. Butchers' offal, chandlers' greaves, and such food, causes the pork to be rank, and should never be given.

In country places, a valuable stock of food can be often got together at a small cost, by giving the women and children of a village a shilling per bushel for all the acorns they can pick up. Some object to the use of acorns on account of its making the flesh hard, but acorns may be given to great advantage, if their use is discontinued before the pigs are shut up for fattening ; and they will be found almost as good as corn for strong and hearty store-pigs.

132. FATTENING.—Pigs are usually fattened with barley-meal mixed into a thin paste with water ; and are often taken from a store condition and put upon this food at once, which is an excellent food, but costs a good deal of money. The most economical way, however, is to make a gradual commencement in the improve-ment of the quality of food, and begin by giving them boiled pota-toes mixed with a little meal, gradually increasing the quantity of the latter till it is given wholly.

By this means the expense is considerably lessened while the pig is approaching the fat condition by progressive stages; and each heightening, as it were, of the quality of the food gives a renewed stimulant towards the fattening process. Bran, and pollard, may be usefully given in conjunction with potatoes at the early stage of fattening, to bring down the gross cost of the food; and by attention to such details as these, pigs may be fattened at a considerably less cost than by the method ordinarily pursued of putting them upon the best food at once, and keeping them to it continuously.

To hogs of large size, peas, or corn bruised, may be given in addition with advantage.

When pigs are being fattened, the most scrupulous cleanliness should be practised, and not more food given at a time than the pig will lick clean up, as none should be left in the trough to stand or get sour; and should there be any left at times, this should be emptied out, and given to the other pigs. The attendant will soon find out how much each animal will eat, and lazily lick the trough for the little that remains adhering to its sides ; and they should be fed at least three times a-day, and a little salt put into their food.

Linseed, which has been recommended by some writers, should never be given to pigs, as it makes the flesh rank in flavour. Nothing, indeed, can excel barley-meal as a food for fattening pigs, the only drawback being its great expense; but this can be kept down, as described, by the free use of potatoes, or by starting off with a mixture of pollard and potatoes, or even bran (assimilation of food being a great point in all feeding), when the pig is first shut up for fattening.

Pigs, as a rule, do not fatten well before they are fifteen months old, except in the case of certain special breeds that have been described, especially well suited for becoming porkers.

March and October are the best times for pigs to come round when fattened, which will allow of fresh-cured bacon to come into use all the year round ; and pigs are never killed during the heats of summer, and the duration of time consumed in the process of fattening is usually from six weeks to two or three months, some breeds fattening much more quickly than others. Anything like the poor Irishman's pig, that took two years to fatten, will prove a decided loss.

While they are being fattened, the pigs should be kept warm ; a certain amount of food being always consumed by all animals for the mere purpose of keeping up the animal heat.

133. RINGING.—In order to prevent pigs from turning up the ground with their noses when turned abroad, or even rooting up the floors of their styes, it is necessary to *ring* them with a ring of iron, which is fixed in the snout of the pig when young, and the tenderness this occasions when it is pressed hardly upon the ground deprives the animal of the power of doing mischief. Some have effected this by cutting the two tendons of the snout about an inch-and-a-half from the nose, which it is said may be done without prejudice to the animal when about two or three months old.

134. SLAUGHTERING.—Pigs are usually stuck in the neck with a knife—the pig-killers who perform this office, and cut up a pig, charging about eighteen-pence, and performing the job with wonderful celerity; but the quickest and mildest way is to use a kind of hammer, or small pole-axe, having a handle about three feet long, and a kind of spike about three inches long at the head. A smart blow struck with this spike on the part of the brain immediately under the curl of hair on the forehead, will cause the pig to die instantly. The aorta must then be immediately opened, to let out the blood, and in this way several pigs can be killed in a few minutes.

The carcase is then scalded on a board or "cratch," by having pailfuls of scalding water thrown over it, taking care the water does not half-cook the outside of the pig, but it should be sufficiently hot to cause the hair to come off freely when scraped with a knife.

When this is done it should be hung up in a cool place, opened, and the entrails taken out, cleansed, and left for at least twelve or fifteen hours. The pig before being slaughtered should be kept without food for twenty-four hours, but plenty of water should be allowed to it in the mean time.

135. **PIG-STYES AND PIGGERIES.**—Pig-styes are often but of
very humble pretensions, and a pig can be made comfortable upon
very slender accommodation, if arranged upon right principles.
The pig-stye should always face the south, and he should be kept
warm, so as not to feel the influence of atmospheric changes, pigs
being gifted proverbially with the talent of being able " to see the
wind." That little pigs acutely feel an unfavourable change upon
the advent of a cold or biting wind, is amply evidenced in the
querulous cries they utter upon these occasions.

*This Illustration and the two following ones show some Piggeries in which the
open yard is covered with an iron roof. The doors are either in front or behind.
If preferred, the arrangement may be reversed, putting the feeding troughs at the
back under cover, in which case the brick houses should be widened so as to pro-
vide a covered feeding passage as shown. These illustrations are kindly lent us
by the St. Pancras Iron Work Company.*

Wherever the stye is put, it should be placed upon a slight elevation, so as to allow of sufficient drainage, and on no account should
it be allowed to remain in a condition of liquid mud of various
consistencies, as may be often seen, under a mistaken idea that a
dirty condition is the natural one for a pig; and upon whatever
scale the accommodation for swine may be fixed, as respects
the number of animals to be kept, each stye should be about
fourteen feet long and seven feet broad, the back portion to be
covered in with a low roof; sufficiently spacious for a large sow or
fatting hog to turn about comfortably in. Sometimes the sleeping

apartment is left open in front, which is a very good plan in sum-mer, but not warm enough in winter, the best method being to have boards to run in a groove at top and bottom, which may be used or taken away at pleasure, a small framework being made to form a doorway. This arrangement will be found much better than making the front of the stye a fixture, as the boards can be taken away and replaced when the inner stye wants cleaning out, and pre-vents the necessity of a man's stooping down to creep through a small hole, which is often the occasion of a stye not being properly cleansed and kept clean.

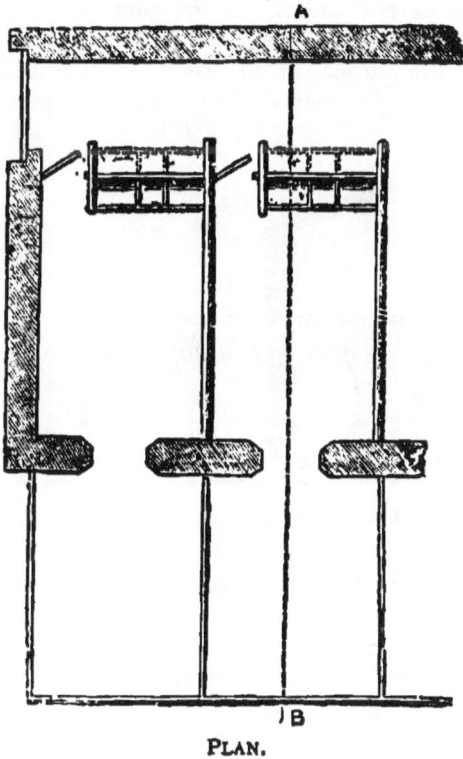

PLAN.

The uncovered part where the animal is fed should be surrounded by a low paling, or low wall, which admits plenty of sun and air. A trough should be placed in front for the reception of the food, with bars across, so that where there is a litter, or several store pigs are shut up together, the stronger ones should not be able to push the weaker ones away with their snouts by thrusting them violently forward, which they will sometimes do.

The method cannot well be adopted where there is a thick wall, but where there is only a paling, it is better to have the food-trough outside, with holes large enough to admit one pig's head. There is a double advantage in this arrangement, for only one pig can occupy a hole at a time, and when one animal, even if he is but a little fellow, has possession of a hole, it is somewhat hard work for another to dislodge him, while the greediness of the would-be monopo-liser of the whole trough, in his anxiety to feed, hastens off to an empty hole, and so leaves the one he has tried to molest in quiet possession. This is one advantage.

Another is, that when a man has to pour wash from a pail into a trough inside, the pigs, in their eagerness, get their heads in the way, or crowd near the pail in such a manner that a good deal is spilled over them at times, and much of the food wasted.

When the troughs cannot be placed outside, hinged shutters, locally termed "witches," are sometimes fixed before them, in order to prevent the pigs putting their feet in them, which yield to the pressure of the snout when he is feeding, but close upon his withdrawing his head.

A few styes, where a number of pigs are kept, should be of larger dimensions, to accommodate several animals of the same age. If water can be conveniently laid on, it will be found of great advantage to have a pipe both for the purpose of cleansing the styes and of mixing the food, which will save a good deal of trouble at times,

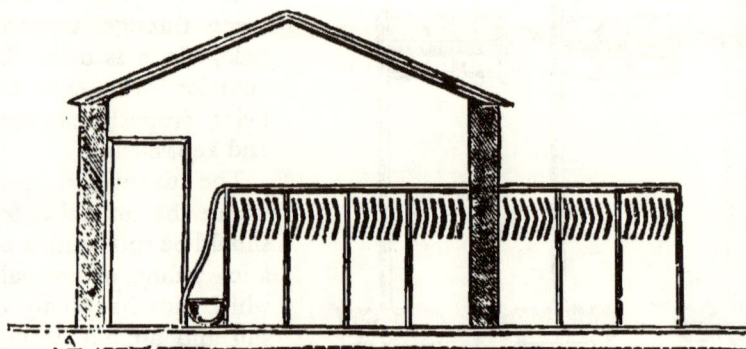

SECTION THROUGH A B ON PLAN.

though "wash," however poor, is always preferable to water for mixing pigs' victuals.

When piggeries are required upon a large scale, a boiling-house should be constructed in the centre, and the styes arranged in a half-circular manner around it, or they may be extended to any length, and a cesspool should be sunk for the liquid manure to run in, which will be found very valuable.

Many very complete buildings have been erected for the accommodation of pigs, but, as a rule, they are a good deal overlooked as profitable stock; many farmers not being able to make them pay when food has to be purchased for them, or they consume food from off the farm which might be sold for so much ready money; but this arises more from defective or bad management, than from any fault connected with the race of animals themselves.

If conveniently arranged, one man could attend to a great number of pigs; Arthur Young having been said to have fattened eighty-eight hogs in one spring, with the attendance of only one man ; the buildings having been arranged in a semicircular fashion.

With economical feeding, and well-arranged piggeries, swine can be made very profitable stock, and valuable adjuncts in a farm, from the vast quantity of manure they can be made the means of manufacturing, with proper and judicious management.

136. BREEDING.—Swine are capable of breeding at eight or nine months, but the boar should be at least twelve months old before he is admitted to the sow, which will also bring a stronger litter if kept back till the same age, and one boar should not be allowed to serve more than ten sows.

137. PERIOD OF GESTATION.—The period of gestation is from sixteen to twenty weeks, the term being extremely various in many species. According to the experiments of M. Teissier, the extreme short and long periods of twenty-five sows were 109 and 143 days ; and as sows can bring two litters a year, it is considered best to arrange the time of farrowing so that it may take place about the latter end of March or early in April ; or towards the end of August ; which lessens the chance of losing young pigs through cold weather, and they require less feeding. The sow, as she approaches her time of farrowing, should be kept tolerably well, in order to be able to supply her young with a proper amount of nourishment, and particularly well fed two or three days before the expected time, which is indicated by her carrying straws in her mouth to form her bed.

138. SOWS DESTROYING THEIR YOUNG.— It sometimes happens that at the first farrowing a sow will eat her young ones, and in order to guard against this happening, the practice is recommended of washing the backs of newly farrowed pigs with a sponge dipped in an infusion of aloes and water, which will prevent her from destroying them ; and about the time of farrowing sows should always be carefully watched.

139. LITTERING SOWS.—The sow should be lodged dryly and warmly, and be well littered up, but the straw should be cut short, to prevent the pigs from nestling under it, in which case the sow is apt to overlay them ; and if a heavy animal, with a large litter, this is pretty sure to happen if this precaution is neglected. The average number of pigs in the first litter is from seven to eight, but it is not always the most numerous litters that are the best ones, as in large litters there are very often several weakly specimens.

140. REARING.—About a week after farrowing, all going on well-

H

the sow may be permitted to leave her sty for a short time every day, and when the little ones are sufficiently strong, they may also accompany her to some orchard or enclosure, keeping them away from the farm yard, where at times they might stand a chance of being smothered, the herbage of a green field improving the quality of a sow's milk; while the pigs will grow faster from the enjoyment of the air and exercise.

141. SUCKING-PIGS.—If the litter is numerous, the number should be lessened, and some killed off as sucking-pigs, which will be best done when they are about three weeks old, by which time the others intended to be raised will be able to follow the sow about, when the males may be castrated; but the spaying of the females should be delayed for another week.

It is generally thought that seven, or at most nine, is a sufficient number of pigs to rear, as it is a great tax upon the sow's power of nourishment to suckle a greater number; and it is best to have fewer strong healthy pigs, which of course would be selected to be kept, and the less strong ones disposed of as sucking-pigs, than rear a large number of weakly pigs.

142. WEANING.—When it is proposed to wean pigs, they should be fed with a little warm skimmed milk, mixed with a small quantity of meal, during the sow's absence; but even her presence will be immaterial, if a small trough is placed in a corner of the stye, with a strong hurdle fastened before it, or a framework of wood, to which the sow cannot obtain access by reason of her size.

They will very soon learn to feed themselves and be independent of the mother, if need be, generally being strong enough for weaning in six weeks' or two months' time, when they should be gradually separated from the sow, and only allowed to suck her twice a-day at first, and once a-day afterwards, leaving the weakest ones a few days longer with their mother.

The young pigs should be taught to feed themselves as early as possible while sucklers, by adopting the contrivance, before spoken of, of having some skimmed milk, butter-milk, or a little good wash, with meal in it, made luke warm, put in a corner for them to have access to, by which the operation of weaning will be very much facilitated.

In concluding our notice of pig-keeping, we may here remark that, under a system of good management and proper attention, few animals can be kept to greater profit or advantage than pigs upon a general farm, if the proper precautions are taken for en-

suring them a supply of food at a small cost, or rather, of turning
those things to account which cost nothing beyond the value of
the labour of their collection, and if it is made a matter of business
to purchase at a small cost any kind of food that can be utilized.

The sweepings of markets or granaries—even malt-dust—is an
excellent thing, when sprinkled over boiled vegetables or green
stuff, that will be benefited by such an admixture; damaged
grain or rice, and the other articles we have mentioned, all can be
made to come in most usefully for pigs.

It is more than probable, too, that the farmers of the future will

pay more attention to the growth of vegetables, and be to a greater
extent *market-gardeners*, there being a large and profitable demand
for vegetables; and upon the refuse of these a large number of
pigs can be cheaply maintained, in addition to other sources of
supply.

Pigs can be put anywhere—in any corner: and keeping them as stock does
not demand any special capabilities of soil, position, or other requirements, as
is the case with other kinds of stock; and they are stock that may be said to be
well in hand, it being possible to keep a great number or a few, according to
circumstances, and the facilities which exist for feeding them; though a contrary
opinion is often found to be entertained, especially by those who are in the
habit of constantly sending to the miller or the cornchandler, in order to satisfy
the appetite of these hearty eaters, instead of taking off its edge with the large
amount of rough stuff that is to be found on every farm, which, with a little
management, can be converted into a large amount of nutritious aliment by the
admixture of a small quantity of concentrated food, the manure they make
lessening considerably the necessity of purchasing, at a high cost, expensive
artificial manures.

WESTPHALIAN PIG.

CHAPTER XI.

PIGS (*continued*).

Diseases and their Remedies—Rheumatism—Catarrh, or Cold—Eruptions of the Skin—Scrofula—The Epidemic—Inflammation of the Chest and Lungs—Protusion of the Rectum—Inflammation of the Bowels—Diarrhœa—Diseases of the Spleen—Colic, or Spasm of the Bowels—Inflammation of the Brain—Gargut—Quinsy, or Strangles—Measles—Leprosy and the Murrain—Mange—Small pox.

143. **DISEASES AND THEIR REMEDIES.**—Pigs are not subject to nearly so long a list of diseases as some of our other domesticated animals; but, from their nature, the symptoms of any derangement are generally very obscure, and diseases often make a good deal of progress before they are discovered; but a good many of these are produced by neglect and want of proper attention.

144. **RHEUMATISM.**—Rheumatism is, perhaps, one of the most common disorders of swine, and is mostly brought about by damp and unwholesome lodging, or exposure to cold; the stye, perhaps, being in too exposed a situation, or placed on damp, undrained ground. A stye on a slight elevation will, with proper means of drainage, be a good safeguard against this disorder, coupled with some warm litter for bedding—pigs, to do well, requiring to be kept warm.

Two to five grains of colchicum, given daily for three or four days, will be found the best medicine for this disease, the bowels being well opened also; but by giving the pigs a good warm stye, and plenty of bedding, and protecting them from keen and biting winds, to which these animals are very averse, rheumatism may be guarded against pretty effectually.

145. **CATARRH, OR COLD.**—Wet, or exposure to the weather, brings on catarrh very often with pigs—the best-cared-for animals being the most exempt—the symptoms being a cough and a mucous discharge from the nostrils. Proper care and good housing are the first steps towards a cure; but when the animal is evidently a good deal affected, it will be found of advantge to administer the following for several successive days :—

Antimonial powder	3 to 6 grains.
Nitre..	10 „ 30 „
Digitalis	1 „ 2 „

When the disorder extends to the lungs, and becomes bronchitis, a more serious phase is entered upon. The animal should then be bled, and a stimulant rubbed on the brisket.

146. **ERUPTIONS OF THE SKIN.**—Pigs suffer occasionally from eruptions of the skin, which usually break out first at the ears, and proceed from opposite causes at times.

A high state of living, when too much heating food is given, will require to be modified by a change of diet, beans and peas being a description of food that has a heating tendency, and when arising from this cause, a cooling lotion should be applied, consisting of the following :—

Muriate of ammonia	4 drachms.
Acetic acid.....................................	1 oz.
Cold water.....................................	1 pint.

Want of air and attention to cleanliness, as well as poor living, will, however, produce the same appearances; and, if not attended to, will spread from the ears over the body in cutaneous pustules, which itch violently and eventually turn into scabs. When the first symptoms make themselves manifest, which will be known by the pigs scratching themselves, if an ounce of sulphur and nitre is mixed with their food, it will be found beneficial. In the large, long-eared breeds the neck and ears become ulcerated; when a mixture of mutton suet and tar, melted together, to which is added a small quantity of the flour of sulphur, should be applied to the affected parts every third day.

If this is not efficacious, the animal should be separated from the rest, and washed thoroughly with strong soap-ley; and ointment of a similar kind occasionally should be applied to the affected parts of the body.

147. **SCROFULA.**—Scrofula is found to affect pigs that are bred too much in and in, finely-bred pigs being the most subject to the disease. Tubercles form in the lungs and mlsentery, which interferes in the case of the latter with the proper absorption of the chyle; nothing in the way of medical treatment being of any avail, till at length the animal dwindles away and dies. The infusion of fresh blood in a stock of pigs is the best preventive.

148. THE EPIDEMIC. — This disorder attacks pigs as well as other animals, the indications being lameness of the feet, caused by soreness between the claws, and the usual inflammation of the substance connecting the bone with the horn, which causes the hoof to be cast when pus has been formed; there being a considerable amount of fever in the system.

Cooling medicine should be given, such as Epsom salts, and an astringent applied to the feet, like that used for sheep affected with sheep-rot. A good astringent is made of a saturated solution of sulphate of copper or zinc.

149. INFLAMMATION OF THE CHEST AND LUNGS. — Pigs that are compelled to lie in damp and wet places are frequently attacked by inflammation of the lungs. Bleeding is generally thought necessary, whether the disorder incline either to bronchitis or pleurisy. The symptoms are quick breathing, a diminished appetite, and fever.

Bleeding is generally recommended as a first step, the bowels being moderately opened by aperient medicine, and the following given once a-day:—

Nitre...	5 to 20 grains.
Calomel	1 „ 3 „
Tartarised antimony	1 „ 3 „

The calomel should be omitted after two doses have been taken. Blisters may also be applied with advantage to the chest.

150. PROTRUSION OF THE RECTUM.—Pigs that are kept upon animal food, and are confined in close, unhealthy quarters, as in the yards of butchers in towns, are the most likely to be visited with this disease, which is also sometimes brought on by violence, or by hunting an animal about, being most frequent with young pigs, and often ending fatally.

The proper treatment for these cases is to keep the pig in a clean, quiet place, and give no food but a little milk, in order to get the bowels well emptied before the gut is put back.

As pigs are rather difficult patients to deal with, after being properly secured, the parts should be washed carefully, and the rectum returned, being pushed up some little distance. Some strong thread should then be tied through the anus, and fastened securely, and no solid food should be given for several days; milk alone being used.

151. INFLAMMATION OF THE BOWELS.—Unwholesome food is the most frequent occasion of inflammation of the bowels, which may be either acute, or sub-acute, the pain being considerable in the former case, without intermission. There is a considerable degree of fever, and loss of appetite, the symptoms being of a more modified character in sub-acute cases, but both being very dangerous.

Bleeding is recommended from the inside of the fore-arm, blood varying in volume from 2 oz. to 2 lb. (according to circumstances) being taken away.

Linseed oil or some other purgative should be given, and in case of severe constipation, injections should be used, and warm baths are also very efficacious, especially in the case of small pigs. Calomel and opium combined, in doses of two to five grains of each, is considered the best medicine for inflammation of the bowels.

Jalap is a good medicine for constipation when there is no active inflammation, given in doses of a scruple to a drachm. Infusion of senna, Glauber salts, and Epsom salts may also be given in the form of a drink. As there is often a difficulty in giving medicine to a pig, linseed oil, which the animal will commonly drink of its own accord, will be found a very useful purgative.

152. DIARRHŒA.—When diarrhœa goes on unchecked for some time, it often assumes a dangerous form in the pig, and turns to inflammation. Prompt treatment is therefore called for, which must be persevered with continually, while the symptoms last, and the following medicine given :—

Powdered opium	15 grains.
Prepared chalk	4 drachms.
Powdered ginger	1 ,,
Peppermint water	4 ounces.

which will be enough to make eight doses.

Should the evacuation be slimy, a dose of Epsom salts should also be given.

153. DISEASES OF THE SPLEEN.—These are very difficult to cure, and the chances of success very remote, the forms being rupture and inflammation, denoted by foaming at the mouth and grinding of the teeth. In cases of rupture they end fatally, while inflammation of the spleen is very dangerous. Bleeding and purging are the only remedies; but there is but slender hopes of good results from treatment except in the milder cases of inflammation.

154. COLIC, OR SPASM OF THE BOWELS—This is a somewhat rare disease with pigs, but occasionally is met with. Medicine is in the first place given, consisting of from 1 drachm to 8 of tincture of opium, and twice that quantity of spirit of nitrous ether,

according to the size of the pig, given in a few ounces of hot water. If this does not afford relief, bleeding must then be resorted to.

155. INFLAMMATION OF THE BRAIN.—The symptoms of inflammation of the brain are dulness, sometimes violent convulsions, and occasionally blindness. Purging and blood-letting are the remedies.

156. GARGUT.—Gargut is an inflammatory affection of the udder of the sow, which being distended by coagulated milk, obstructs the lacteal ducts. Too rich feeding before the time of farrowing sometimes produces it, the treatment being in slight cases to bathe the bag with camphorated spirits of wine. As the young pigs will not suck the vitiated milk, it should be gently pressed out by the hand, but if it cannot be extracted by this means, it will be best to kill the sow.

157. QUINSY, OR STRANGLES.—Fat hogs are the most liable to this disease; the throat swelling, and the pulse and breathing being greatly accelerated, which ends in suffocation if relief is not afforded. The tongue protrudes, and is covered with slaver, and gangrene follows unless the progress of the disorder is arrested by bleeding and purging.

158. MEASLES.—Pigs are sometimes attacked by measles, though they are seldom fatal, measly pork being not uncommon, and occasionally sold to the poor in third-rate shops, the meat having a faded appearance, and the flesh punctured with small holes, or distensions of the fibre, which is caused by a number of small watery pustules externally.

Cooling medicines, such as Epsom salts and nitre, are generally efficacious, the symptoms being fever, cough, discharge from the nostrils, and pustules under the tongue.

159. LEPROSY, AND THE MURRAIN.—Leprosy is a formidable disease, but very seldom met with in this country; but the murrain —a species of leprosy—is caused by inflammation of the blood in hot seasons; the best preventive being to keep the pigs cool, and not give them any heating food, such as animal refuse.

160. MANGE.—Pigs are much less subject to mange than dogs, horses and sheep, though it is occasionally met with, the symptoms being the usual itching. Sulphur ointment, mercurial ointment, or tobacco-water, well rubbed in the skin, are the best remedies to have recourse to.

161. SMALL-POX.—Small pox is extremely rare in the case of pigs, though they are occasionally attacked by this disease.

Regularity in feeding, and perfect cleanliness are the best safe-guards against attacks of disease of all kinds, and, as prevention is better than cure, if a small quantity of nitre and sulphur is occasionally mixed up with their food, it will often prevent disease, keep them cool, and yet be the means of giving a healthy stimulus to their appetite.

CASHMERE GOATS.

SYRIAN GOATS.

CHAPTER XII.

GOATS.

Natural History—Varieties—Statistics relating to Goats in England—Uses—
Goat's Hair—As Food—Goat's-Milk Cheese—The Skin—Uses in Foreign
Countries—Management—Tethering—Breeding—Diseases.

162. **NATURAL HISTORY.**—As mentioned before in reference
to the sheep, the goat so closely resembles the latter that some
naturalists have regarded them as one and the same species; the
difference between them being so very trifling as scarcely to be
noticeable, the only distinct variation being the presence of the
interdigital hole, or gland, which is found in one animal, but not in
the other.

Those who disagree with this view have pointed to the hairy coat
of the goat, which more resembles the hide of the ox than the wool
of the sheep; but it is noticeable that, in cold climates, the wool of
the sheep becomes nearly allied in its character to *hair*, while the
hair of the goat in warmer latitudes partakes more of the nature of
wool.

This fact has been brought strikingly forward in the case of the
late Sir Titus Salt, of Bradford, who was the first to manufacture

the bright-haired wool of the alpaca into dress-stuffs in this country
—fabrics that got to be world-renowned, and were turned out in
vast quantities in his manufactory at Saltaire, near Bradford.

When Pizarro first reached Peru, the natives were found in
possession of two domesticated animals, the llama, and the alpaca,
and he and his companions were at a loss whether to consider
them as camels or sheep; but finding as they advanced into the
interior that large flocks were kept, and the wool was used for
clothing, the Spaniards dubbed them *Carneros de la tierra*, or
country sheep.

The softness of the wool of the llama has long been renowned, of
which the Spanish naturalist Acosta gave the first description in his
work, *Historia Natural y Moral de Las Indias*, published in 1590, the
alpaca bearing a heavy fleece, and the llama bearing but a short
coat.. The story of Sir Titus Salt haviug cursorily noticed a lot of
neglected alpaca wool lying in a corner of a Liverpool merchant's
warehouse, and the large branch of industry which originated from
his clever manipulation of it, giving employment to thousands of
workmen in this country, is generally well known.

As a proof of .the close affinity between the sheep and the goat,
the fact has been pointed out that the hybrids produced from the
cross between a goat and an ewe have not been barren, but, according to Cuvier, (*Règne Animal, tome* 1, *p.* 277), have not only been productive, but prolific.

Mountain sheep in a state of nature bear a close affinity to goats,
being, according to Wilson, both " Alpine animals, fearless of crag
and cliff, and dwelling, indeed, by preference amongst the steepest
and most inaccessible summits of lofty mountains."

163. **VARIETIES.**—The varieties of the goat, as we are acquainted
with the race in England, are somewhat circumscribed; but a
greater difference exists amongst goats, perhaps, in individual
instauces, than amongst any other class of domestic animals, with
respect to their productiveness, some not giving more than an
English pint of milk daily, while others will give as much as four
quarts.

As goats might often be kept very profitably, provided the right
kind of animal is selected, those chosen should be of the largest
size, with hard, stiff hair, but in not too great quantity, with a form
of neck resembling that of the sheep, with small head—those not
furnished with horns generally turning out the best milkers.

. Light colours, such as pied, or light yellow, should be avoided, and preference given to those that are of a dark hue, approaching black as nearly as possible.

164. STATISTICS RELATING TO GOATS IN ENGLAND.—There do not appear to be any very accurate statistics furnished as to the number of goats in England, sheep and goats generally being classed together, but a society has lately been formed with the object of drawing a greater amount of public attention to the utility of the goat, which under proper management can be made a profitable animal, well worthy the attention of farmers and stock-keepers.

165. USES.—The goat in this country is not put to so many or profitable uses as 't is abroad ; a few of which we will speak of.

166. GOAT'S HAIR.—Goat's hair is largely used in some Eastern countries in the manufacture of many textile fabrics; certain kinds of shawls and other articles being manufactured from it, but principally used in an admixture with wool. Many beautiful and fanciful fabrics that are imported to us from India have a considerable quantity of goat's hair woven up in them. Ropes made of goat's hair are very durable and will bear all weathers, never rotting from moisture. The hair is clipped annually about the middle of May.

167. AS FOOD.—A great prejudice exists against the use of the flesh of the goat or kid in this country as an article of food, which is scarcely warranted. In a good many southern countries, notably in the Peninsula, the flesh of the kid is as regularly served at table as lamb, and by a good many who partake thereof considered the better of the two. The flavour of the flesh of the kid has none of that rankness which is peculiar to goat's flesh, which is commonly eaten by the peasantry in some southern countries as a staple article of meat diet; being very similar to mutton but stronger tasted, and commonly eaten both in Spain and Portugal as a regular dish.

The produce of the goat in the form of milk is often very useful in the case of invalids, being light and nutritious ; a good deal of it being sold under the name of goat's whey, strongly resembling cow's milk in flavour.

168. GOAT'S-MILK CHEESE.—Goat's-milk cheese is another article of diet that is constantly made and eaten abroad in those southern countries where goats are numerous and flocks of them regularly kept; forming a constant portion of the evening meal, in the same way that ordinary cheese is eaten in England.

169. THE SKIN.—The skin of the goat is very valuable for the purpose of making shoes and "kid" gloves, as they are termed, of

which only an insufficient supply can be obtained, the demand for
them ever increasing, not only in this country but abroad, and
especially in America; large quantities of kid gloves being sold
every year in New York. In France, for a length of time they have
been a special article of commerce. Lamb's skin is often used as a
substitute; a great many more lamb's-skin gloves being disposed of

ALPACA GOAT.

under the name of kid, than kid itself, which is of firmer grain and
texture and retains its shape better, being what is technically called
a "better fit."

170. USES IN FOREIGN COUNTRIES.—It will thus be seen
that in foreign countries the goat is utilised to a considerably
greater degree than in England, the milk being largely used also
in the form of cheese, while the flesh of the kid is eaten as a deli-

cacy, like lamb, and that of the goat in the place of mutton. Kid skins are a valuable article of commerce; and there can be no question but their use and profit in this country could be largely extended under proper management.

171. MANAGEMENT.—At one time goats were kept to a con-siderable extent in Wales, but their numbers have been steadily diminishing in favour of sheep, and the generally higher condition of agriculture which now obtains; though agriculture is in a very backward condition comparatively in those parts of the Principality where goats would be most likely to be kept, mountainous regions being particularly well suited to their habits.

There are many heathy wild spots upon which goats could be kept to great pecuniary advantage, and a large amount of profit might be obtained from the milk and kids.

A main reason why sheep have been preferred to goats of late years has been, doubtless, owing to the Enclosure Acts, the enclo-sure of land having been the means of banishing them from many parts, as they nip the hedges and leap over high fences; and thus, in their native condition, as it may be said, it is somewhat difficult to keep them within bounds.

Doubtless the keeping of sheep and pigs would always be more satisfactory to the great majority of agriculturists than keeping goats would prove, but there are situations where other animals could not be sustained, upon which the goat would thrive.

172. TETHERING.—It is not generally known, and is against what would be the common supposition, but nevertheless it is a fact, that a goat will give more milk when tethered to a certain spot than when allowed to roam about at will. The tether should be attached to an iron pin, driven into the ground by a swivel, to prevent the entanglement of the chain, and the position of this peg should be shifted two or three times a-day, in order to allow the goat to browse upon fresh herbage when required.

173. BREEDING.—A goat breeds but once a-year, going to the buck in December, and producing kids in April, the she-goat invariably bringing two and sometimes three kids, and will give milk all the year round up to within a few weeks of parturition.

The kids should only be allowed to suck for a week, and then be disposed of to the butcher; and it may safely be affirmed that if the flesh of kids were regularly furnished to our markets, that a taste for it could be made to spring up amongst the ordinary meat-eaters of the kingdom; an unnatural prejudice only keeping it out

of the market. In the Mosaic accounts we are often told of the
hospitality of the patriarchs, who killed a kid for the entertainment
of their guests, and of the touching account of Isaac's blessing
obtained by Jacob to the disparagement of poor Esau, whose anger
against his brother was certainly justified by the fraud practised
upon him.

A goat is considered at its best at the ages inclusive between
three and six years; and the she-goat generally goes to the buck
when six or nine months old. As the amount of milk she gives
with her first kid is comparatively small, it is better to allow her to
suckle it, as it will increase her supply of milk, and cause her to be
much more productive during the ensuing year.

174. **DISEASES.**—The diseases of goats are comparatively few;
and very likely it would be the same with many of our other
domesticated animals, did they but live in a condition more
resembling their natural state, as intended by nature, and not in an
artificial one; and to the greater freedom and liberty enjoyed by the
goat, as well as to its natural hardihood, must be attributed this
fortunate immunity.

THE MULE.

CHAPTER XIII.

ASSES AND MULES.

Natural History—The Ass—The Mule—Hinnys—Breeding—Diseases—Uses.

175. **NATURAL HISTORY.**—There is some little doubt as to the exact origin of the ass in this country, and from what breed or animal he has descended; the common supposition being that it is of Eastern origin, which owed its original existence to a commixture of the wild ass, which appears under somewhat different forms in various lands; there being numerous tribes of wild asses that roam the desert, some peculiar to the warm plains of Persia, and others in less genial districts, as the south of Russia; while another species is common to the Arabian deserts, a swift and handsomer animal, that in a state of liberty offers a lively contrast to that patient drudge known as the English "donkey," which is often so cruelly used, and so contemptuously spoken of, but which, under kind and rational treatment, is capable of being converted into a most useful, and intelligent servant.

176. **THE ASS.**—Hollinshed says that "our land did yield no asses in the time of Queene Elizabeth," but in this he was wrong, because in the early history of England they are stated to have been abundant in the reign of Ethelred, A.D. 870, and their second introduction is stated to be due to James the First of England and Sixth of Scotland.

I

The asses known in England, in their present condition, are a very inferior kind; but this is no doubt chiefly due to the utter neglect into which this race of animals has fallen; and if some skilful breeder were but to turn his attention to them, and bestow as much pains as has been given to the improvement of our other domesticated animals, doubtless a much more valuable breed would be obtained.

Asses which have been reared in the island of Gozo, in the Mediterranean, some of which have been brought over to England as

THE ASS.

stallions for the production of mules, have reached the height of fourteen hands.

In Spain there is to be found a very fine breed of asses, a good deal of attention being paid to them, with the view to their utility in the production of mules, the Spaniards making pets of them, and treating them with kindness and consideration.

It is surprising that asses are not made more use of by farmers in England, considering their useful nature, and the small cost of their living; for any picking contents the poor donkey, who will satisfy himself with the leavings of other cattle, and be content with tufts of rank and bitter grass, that none other will eat, and pick up his living in any bye-lane.

As a draught animal, two donkeys will do as much work as a horse, and in many ways their power of usefulness and general service might be easily much increased, by more considerate and better treatment than they are in the habit of getting generally, being more hardy in constitution, more patient, and more muscular in proportion to their weight than horses; and are also less subject to disease, and live longer, the duration of the life of an ass being often forty years, and although horses sometimes attain even that age, the instances are very rare.

177. **THE MULE.**—Some writers have described the mule to be the issue produced by horses upon she-asses, and the progeny of the jackass and the mare irrespectively. But this is a mistake, the hybrids produced in these two separate ways being altogether different animals. The mule bred between the ass and the mare is a very superior animal, partaking more of the nature of the horse than of the ass, except in ear and tail, being a large, swift and sure-footed animal; and, when carefully bred, is a superior animal to both of his parents, as he possesses the stature, beauty, and paces of the horse (sometimes standing sixteen hands high, good specimens being worth fifty and sixty pounds in Spain, where they are ridden by noblemen of the highest rank at times), and possessing the patience and endurance of the ass, together with its great comparative strength.

The best mules are produced by a Spanish ass upon an English thoroughbred mare, but it is quite evident that if some farmers would raise mules by crossing indifferent mares with a good Spanish jackass, the result would be a race of animals far better adapted for farm work where light animals are required, than the poor *screws* that are often seen; this remark of course applying to those third-rate attempts at breeding horses that may be occasionally witnessed.

178. **HINNYS.**—The hybrid produced by the horse upon the she-ass is an inferior animal to the mule, called a "hinny," and in some districts locally a "mute," and in Ireland a "gennatin," and is different to the mule both in size and form. This is easily accounted for by the greater capacity of the mare for carrying a larger animal in accordance with well-known laws in breeding, the "hinny" being much smaller and less robust than the mule, and of course far less valuable.

This distinction seems to be but little understood by many writers, even by so high an authority as Buffon, who apparently considered it to have been the product arising from the union of the ox and the mare.

179. BREEDING.—The she-ass carries her young a few days over eleven months, and the ass-colt does not arrive at full maturity until his fourth or fifth year. In breeding, as good specimens of both male and female should be obtained as possible, and of as large a size as can be got.

The salient points to aim at are: long neck; wide nostrils; eye large and full, with raised withers, full back, and large quarters: and if care is bestowed, and continued, a very superior race of asses could be produced to what are commonly seen in England.

The mule's sterility is of course well known, being incapable of continuing its race ; although there are certain well-authenticated instances to the contrary, it being a maxim of zoology that hybrids are infertile.

180. DISEASES.—The ass is singularly free from disease, being very hardy and capable of bearing any extremes of weather, but subject occasionally to loss of condition arising from colds, chiefly produced by exposure and neglect, which gives way before considerate treatment, warm housing and good food.

Asses have been driven in pony-carriages repeatedly, and trained to do their work as efficiently as ponies; and when well groomed, and well broken, are by no means the despicable animals they are often considered.

181. USES.—Even at his worst the ass is by no means to be despised, and as a beast of burden on a farm, a donkey and cart driven by a boy is capable of performing a large amount of useful service, and could upon many occasions be cheaply substituted for a horse, in carrying light loads to and fro upon a farm ; the exchange in many instances being made with absolute advantage, as the lighter beast and weight of carriage will not cut up the land so much when it is crossed as the heavier horse and cart.

From the bones of the ass the ancients used to make their flutes, or *fibulæ.* In the present day the integuments are used in the manufacture of parchment, and the skin makes excellent leather for shoes—the article used for cases called *shagreen*, or more properly *sagri*, being also made from it ; while the parchment formed from the integument of the ass is considered to form the best material for producing sonorous sounds from that warlike instrument the drum.

INDEX.

J. OGDEN AND CO., PRINTERS, 172, ST. JOHN STREET, E.C,

www.ingramcontent.com/pod-product-compliance
Lightning Source LLC
Chambersburg PA
CBHW030619270326
41927CB00007B/1233